CONTENTS

KU-201-733

1

LOOKING FOR YOUR ANCESTORS

This book assumes that you have no knowledge at all of family history research, that you are a complete but enthusiastic beginner. It will take you step by step through the process of tracing your own family history. I would ask you to read the book through first so that you will have some idea of what you are about to undertake, then to return to the beginning and follow the suggested assignments through, chapter by chapter.

Who are you? You are the present-day accumulation of all the genes, characteristics and hereditary behaviour of your ancestors. Have you ever wondered who your ancestors were, where they lived and what they did? What they looked like?

Heredity is not exclusive to anyone. We all have ancestors and we all have sagas to tell. Everybody can enjoy this hobby. The dustman and the duke, the ordinary person as much as royalty is able equally to research his or her own family history. It is not an area exclusively owned by the nobility although, of course, in the writings of history, opinions as to whose families matter the most will always differ.

Over the past 50 years the growth of this leisure activity, which seems to reflect a romantic nostalgia for the past, has astounded professional researchers. This development has been both beneficial and stimulating. Men and women work at their researches, introducing into what used to be a recreation a certain amount of professionalism. Information has spread worldwide (perhaps because of the ease of communication made available to us by our electronic age) and the chances of finding out more about remote branches of your family are increased because your distant relative, hitherto unknown to you, has also been working away researching his family history and you can exchange your knowledge to each other's benefit.

Become a Detective

In order to research your own family history you will have to be a detective, looking for clues and sifting the evidence available. Perseverance, luck, careful correct copying and note taking are all essential. There can never be a guarantee of success, but you will always find it a challenging and satisfying hobby. It takes time and is a slow process but it is well worth all the effort put into it. With persistence and a degree of luck you will be able to trace your family roots back to the late 1700s and possibly even further. I experienced an extreme example of luck one day when I required the assistance of an American researcher. Using my list of professional researchers, covering the whole of America, and the 'pin' method I wrote to an unknown genealogist in the state where I required a search. The work was quickly and efficiently completed and when the documents were sent to me the letter accompanying them also told me that my professional colleague had an ancestor with the same surname as myself (my husband's family surname) whose family originated in Kent in England. The name is unusual and I was able to confirm that my husband's family did indeed originate in Kent. We discovered later that my husband's family and that of my American colleague were indeed related. The saint of genealogists must certainly have guided my 'pin' that day.

If you can one day show your family a well presented and interesting history they will be delighted. Do not doubt it. You will also gain great satisfaction and pleasure from a job well done and have something to pass on to your children who may well be bitten by the bug and continue the research. It is endless. As members of your family are born, marry or die, so the information to add to your research grows.

Before you begin, go to the library and borrow biographies of famous people. You will find them interesting to read and they will give you some ideas on how to start and what you are looking for. Your own family history is as interesting as anyone else's, whether famous or not. There are also family history societies in existence. Go to a meeting of your local society – your library will probably know where and when they meet or you can find out on their internet website. They will welcome you as a newcomer and give advice and you will meet people who have the same interest as yourself.

Talk to Your Relatives

How and where do you start? First talk to your family and tell them what you are doing. Contact your cousin in Australia or your aunt in Scotland. It may be that others in your family are engaged in family history research and have done some of the work for you. They will produce all sorts of bits and pieces which may prove useful (if not immediately, then perhaps later when they slot into a space and confirm some piece of research which you have been following).

Gather up all the information you can from your family before you start. It may provide clues and help which will save you a great deal of time. Old letters, postcards and birthday cards in particular are very helpful. Articles from newspapers, letters from abroad, wills and diaries can provide dates and names that you are looking for.

Before it is too late, talk to your older relatives and make a note of what they tell you. There is nothing that old people like to do better than talk about 'the old days'. They will, while reminiscing about past events and places, reveal much information to help you. They may need gentle prompting as to exact names, dates and occasions. Don't be afraid to ask them. Encourage them and they will be a mine of information. Personal knowledge will often reveal unknown relationships but they must always be checked and supported by documentation if your family history is to be based on fact.

If you find it difficult to write quickly and keep up with what is being said, invest in a small personal recorder, the type which is not intrusive, which you can hold in your hand or lay on a table. They are not too expensive and you can save all the information to go through at a later date when you have more time. Some people may object to the use of a recorder and 'dry up' but most will soon forget its presence and talk freely. Your only difficulty will be not to miss anything that is being said.

A word of warning, do not take everything that members of your family tell you as fact. They may choose not to tell you about one particular person whom they disliked or with whom they quarrelled or who they consider is a disgrace to the family. There may have been incidents in the past which they do not wish to remember. Memories are often hazy as to dates and places. They are also coloured by happy or sad experiences. Memory plays funny tricks. We all have some things we would rather forget. It may be those very things that you will need to know. Everything should be checked where possible by following up information given. If several members of the family tell the same story it probably is true, but not always. It may have been handed down by tradition and the facts changed by each storyteller to suit the occasion. It is for you to discover the answers.

Family Bibles

Some families have family Bibles in which generations of names and dates have been recorded. Possibly one of your older aunts or a grandparent has it pushed away in a cupboard. Although it is not on display, they will not want to part with it. You may have to copy the entries. If you do, make sure you copy them exactly, even if you think the spelling is incorrect. Sometimes the words can be hard to decipher so ask other members of the family if they remember any of the names. If you have a digital camera, photo the relevant pages. If not, try to persuade the owner to part with the Bible for a short time, so that you can get the pages photocopied. Most towns have 'copy shops' charging a small sum per page for copies. If you return the Bible promptly, the owner will know you are to be trusted and may produce other treasured documents for you to see.

Old Photographs

Old photographs and photograph albums can be a source of much information. Very often notes of the people in the photographs or places and dates where they were taken will be found written on the back. If there was an enthusiastic photographer in the family who kept his work in an album, he probably wrote all the details beside each picture. This could prove a great source of information. Perhaps distant relations are able to email you photographs of family members you have never seen before.

When you have gathered all the available details you should have many pages of your notebook filled, or several recordings waiting to be played at your leisure and you will probably have renewed acquaintance with a few distant relatives who were no doubt very pleased to hear from you.

Family history research can result in many happy reunions with those we thought were lost to us and introductions to those we did not know existed.

Start with Yourself

It is no use jumping into the middle just because you have some odd pieces of information about distant relatives. You can only start with the information about which you are certain, so begin with yourself and work back into the past. If you have an uncommon name or a family name that is passed down from one generation to another, then it will be much easier, but you may find that your name, which you thought was unusual, is in fact very common in some other part of the country. This may be a helpful point of reference but could lead you on a time-consuming and wasteful exercise unless you are sure there is some connection.

Keeping Notes

Remember to keep *all* the notes that you make, even those on scraps of paper and the backs of envelopes. You never know when they may come in useful.

If you are using a computer, transfer all the information you have gathered onto your hard disk, DVD, CD or USB flash device dedicated to your family history. Always make a backup of all your research in case any difficulty arises in retrieving the information you have stored.

It is also essential to make a note of where you obtained the specific pieces of information in case you ever need to check the notes you made or refer again to a particular book or documents. Cite the exact source of the information and give all the data you have at the time you make your notes. If you copy information from the family Bible, it is not sufficient to mark your notes 'from the family Bible'. You may not remember who has possession of the Bible or where it is housed. Make a full note of the date on which the notes were taken, in whose possession the Bible remains and the address. It is particularly important to make a note of your sources of reference when visiting registries, libraries, museums or newspaper archives. You may have spent a great deal of time tracking down the information. The next time you need to refer to it a great deal of wasted time and frustration will be avoided if you know where to look. The following are examples of good and bad reference notes. For the purpose of these examples you are the family historian 'John Smith'.

BAD	GOOD
Letter from Aunt Annie	Letter from Mrs Annie Goodall dated 27 January 2008 to John Smith (family historian). Letter now in possession of John Smith filed under reference G/29.

BAD	GOOD
Family Bible	Copied by John Smith, 19 January 2008, from family Bible record of Arthur Smith of Harrogate b. 2 November 1867. Bible in possession of Harold G. Smith of 22 Grace Street, Harrogate. Original entries in Bible handwritten, authors unknown. Photocopies in possession of John Smith filed under reference S/6.

BAD	GOOD
Book in Guildhall Library	Information copied 2 March 2008 by John Smith from book

'Gleaning History' by S. R. Green. Published by Fish & Sons 2000. Book available at Guildhall Library, London. Library reference No. 86/B7.

BAD

A death certificate

GOOD

Information copied by John Smith 6 May 2008 from death certificate of Constance Ellen Harris d. 29 October 1899. Original in possession of Alice Cross (daughter of C. E. Harris) of 22 Cramery Road, Northampton. Photocopy in possession of John Smith filed under reference H/219.

If you are entering the information on your computer, the same methods should be used. It is essential to know where the information came from.

BAD

Via internet from Aunt Annie

GOOD

Received via email 27 January 2008 from Mrs Annie Goodall (annie@aol.net) copy of letter to John Smith, family historian. Ref: G/29. Original letter in possession of Annie Goodall.

All families do not have 'skeletons in the cupboard' nor a banished 'black sheep' but it is much more interesting if they do. Not many people can boast a highwayman or an illegitimate earl as a distant ancestor, but you may be surprised by the occupations and connections of your forebears. I have met many who through their research claim a family association with the royal family, the Churchill family, one of the great families of Europe or well known American families, however tenuous the link may be. Most families, however, even if they have a tradition of being town dwellers will find roots somewhere in the countryside.

A little like a jigsaw puzzle, start at the outside edges and work inwards as you find the pieces that fit together. It may take a long time to find the one piece that will enable you to proceed further but do not give up. You may lose your way and feel discouraged. You may decide to give up the research for a time, possibly a few months, or even years. It doesn't matter; it is always there for you to return to. The chances are, however, that once you start you will find it difficult to stop. It will be your own personal serial or 'soap opera'; you will feel compelled to know 'what happened next'.

Which Branch to Research?

One more thing to decide before you go any further is which branch of your family you are going to follow first. The further you go, the more branches your family tree will have and those branches will divide into smaller branches and eventually into twigs, each bearing a name and a relationship to the others. If you start with yourself, your family name will usually be the same as that of your father. Before they married, your mother's family name was probably different from that of your father, so that immediately you have two family names to follow. By the time you get to your grandparents you will have four family names to research and when you reach your great-grandparents you will have eight different family names. Fig. 1 gives an illustration.

Most people follow their father's family name when they start, following through with the male line only. This is called

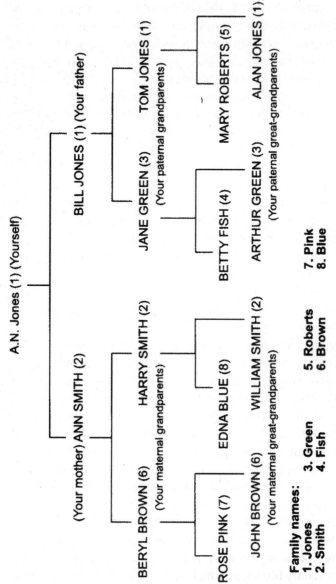

Fig. 1. Family tree as far back as your great-grandparents.

the *paternal line*. If you follow your mother's family, that is your *maternal line*. It is easier to start on your paternal line since you will be following only one surname. Any other names gathered at the same time can be kept and followed later in your research. If you come to a sudden stop with your paternal line because you cannot find the next clue, leave it for a while and follow your maternal line, or branch off on to your paternal grandmother's family. There will always be plenty of other trails to follow.

The Internet

The use of computers and the internet has had the most enormous impact on family history research in recent years, enabling family historians to access historical information from the comfort of their own homes and communicate with distant relatives all over the world.

If you do not have a computer at home, try logging on to the internet at a local library, school, college, friend or neighbour's house or at a cybercafé.

If you do not already possess a computer, or are thinking of upgrading your current one, it may be worthwhile purchasing a laptop computer which you can take with you when you visit record offices, libraries and registries as many of these places now provide facilities for plugging in portable computers.

The internet is one of the fastest growing sources of genealogical information. There are thousands of websites which can help you with your family history research. These include government sites (such as that of The National Archives), family history society sites (such as that of The Society of Genealogists), commercial sites (for example, FindMyPast and Ancestry) where you can access material on a subscription or pay-by-view basis, as well as sites set up by fellow family historians which provide free information (such as FreeBMD). I refer to these sites and others in the book wherever relevant and give their full address details in the Appendix and in the Quick Index to Useful Websites.

Research on the internet will help you to find where original documents are held, when you can visit the various centres and how much it will cost. It will not, however, give you access to *all* the birth, marriage and death records, census records and original documents you will need, although each year more and more information is made available on the web. You may still need to visit The National Archives at Kew, local record offices, museums and libraries if you wish to see the original documents.

There are also social networking websites such as Genes Reunited which help to connect relatives researching the same family. You can upload details of your family to these sites so that others have access to your research and you can gain access to theirs. This can be a great help and enable you to find distant relations you would probably never have found otherwise.

However, you do need to exercise caution when putting your research into the public domain, especially now that identity theft is a common problem in our modern society. Never include a living person's personal details (such as date and place of birth) anywhere on the internet unless you have that individual's express permission. Even if your relatives allow you to do so, consider carefully whether it is really necessary to reveal such information.

Also make sure that you give proper credit to people who have given you information about your family. Don't simply copy someone else's hard work and claim it as your own. Be aware, too, that once your tree is freely accessible to others on the internet, they may copy it without giving you any credit!

It is worth bearing these points in mind before you upload any information. Sometimes new family historians are so fired with enthusiasm that they rush onto these sites and exchange information that they would never reveal to strangers they met in the street.

Always double check information that others give you as they may have made a mistake in their research. Do not accept everything that appears on the internet to be true; others may not be as meticulous in their research as (I hope) you will be.

One of the pleasures of family history research is meeting others who are researching your own family and discussing with them the information that you have discovered. You can exchange tips on where to find information, the best way to research at the various centres, the easiest way to get there, the best times when research space is available, where the toilets are, the nearest eateries and many other helpful facts. If you do most of your research on the internet, although you can exchange information by email and you need never leave home, you may miss out on the companionship of meeting like-minded people.

Family History Courses

The Open University runs a course on family history. The course reference is currently A173 and is intended to help students interpret and write about family history. However, you need computer and internet access to enrol. The course might be of interest to those of you embarking on your own family history for the first time.

There are a number of other courses on beginning genealogy available on the internet and elsewhere if you wish to learn more about the subject in a structured way. Make sure you are happy with the contents of the course and the reputation of the organization running it before you part with any money.

Visiting Record Offices and Archives

Provide yourself with a good notebook and plenty of pencils. Many registries, libraries and archives do not allow the use of ballpoint pens and insist on the use of pencils only. If you make a practice of using pencils everywhere, you can't go wrong. Some record offices, including The National Archives in Kew, even have restrictions on the type of notebook you can take with you while researching their records so before visiting any record office or archive always check the latest rules on what you are allowed to use.

The first thing you will realize when you visit any record office or archive is that you are not alone in your interest in family history research. Most centres are always full of people looking for their ancestry. You will hear Australian, American, West Indian, Canadian, Indian, Scots and Irish accents as well as English. The centres are always crowded with both professional and amateur searchers of all ages. Not all family historians are maiden aunts, retired colonels and housewives; many are young. The one thing they all have in common is enthusiasm. In the summer holiday months the number of searchers is increased by visitors from abroad and students on holiday. Most, but not all, researchers are friendly. They are all absorbed in their own research, but sometimes do not object to being asked for advice – they may even offer it! A delighted cry of 'found it' can often be heard when a dedicated but tired searcher's patience is rewarded. Sympathetic smiles and nods of encouragement will greet that lucky person. Do not be intimidated by obviously experienced searchers – they were all beginners themselves once.

2

BIRTH, MARRIAGE AND DEATH CERTIFICATES (ENGLAND AND WALES)

When you have gathered all the existing information from your family, store it safely and start at the beginning with yourself. Do you have a copy of your own birth certificate? Get it out and look at it. What does it tell you?

Birth Certificates
A full birth certificate (as opposed to a short birth certificate which only includes the name, date of birth, sex and registration district) should give you:

1. A date and place of birth.
2. A name.
3. The sex.
4. The father's name and surname.
5. The mother's name and maiden name (her surname before she was married).
6. The father's occupation.
7. The name and description of the person giving the information of the birth and their address.

8. The date of registration.
9. The district in which the birth was registered.
10. The sub-district in which the birth was registered.
11. The county in which the birth was registered.

From this, you can see how useful such certificates are to family historians, as they link children to their parents and give the names of the previous generation.

If a birth was registered in England or Wales after 1968 the birth certificate will also show the birthplace of both parents and the previous name of the mother if different from her maiden name. If, for instance, she had been widowed or divorced and remarried, then her previous surname would also be given.

Registration of births, deaths and marriages became compulsory in England and Wales on 1 July 1837. Registrars entered the details locally and then every three months (i.e. every quarter) sent copies of the records to the central registry.

The months included in each quarter are:

March quarter entries:	January, February, March
June quarter entries:	April, May, June
September quarter entries:	July, August, September
December quarter entries:	October, November, December

All the entries at the General Register Office (see Appendix) are indexed alphabetically. By searching these indexes you should be able to find the GRO index reference you need to order a copy of a certificate. It should therefore in theory be easy to trace your family history at least back to the dates of compulsory registration with little difficulty. It should be, but it is not always so. That is what makes it so interesting. If it were a matter of simply looking through the indexes with a list of names and dates it would soon become repetitious and boring, but somewhere along the line you will 'lose' someone and you will have to start looking elsewhere. That is when you become a detective and when the information you have gathered from your family can be used as a reference.

For a long time I had 'lost' my paternal grandfather. He was a Londoner and I could not find the registration of his death in any of the London districts. However, on talking to my aunt (his daughter), I discovered that he had been working in Leith in Scotland during the Second World War – she was actually sent there to register his death at that time. With that information, I was able to obtain his death certificate.

Sometimes a birth is registered before a name for the child is chosen and no name will be shown on the certificate. To find the entry for such a birth in the GRO indexes you need to look at the end of the entries for the particular surname where unnamed boys are listed under Male and unnamed girls are listed under Female. Bear this in mind if you cannot find someone in the main alphabetical list and always check the Male and Female entries at the end.

The GRO indexes are now available on the internet so that family historians can search them from their own homes or in local libraries. One particular website which may be of interest to you is the FreeBMD site. Here volunteers have put millions of the GRO birth, marriage and death indexes from 1837 onwards onto the web. At no cost, you can search for your ancestor by name and (if you are lucky enough to find him or her) can obtain the GRO index reference (the district, volume and page reference) needed to order the relevant certificate from the GRO. Other websites where you can search the indexes for free but may need to pay (either by subscription or pay-by-view) to be able to see a scan of the relevant index page containing the GRO reference include Ancestry and FindMyPast.

Microfiche copies of the index are also available at some libraries, local record offices and family history societies, while microfilm copies are available at the family history centres of the Church of Jesus Christ of Latter-day Saints (LDS), see page 133. The drawback of such copies is that sometimes they are difficult to read.

A microfiche is about the size of a large postcard and it is read by inserting the film, flat, into a special machine so that the contents are thrown up onto a screen. The microfiche is moved about, forwards and backwards, to the right or the left, in order to bring into focus the names you are seeking. The microfiche machines are very simple to use.

Some county councils and family history societies (for example, Cambridgeshire and Cheshire) also have combined forces to make available indexes for their particular areas on the internet. These indexes may not yet be complete but they may be useful if they cover the area where your family lived. These websites provide references which enable you to order certificates online or by post from the particular register office where the event was registered.

Remember that registration of an event may not necessarily take place on the same date as the event. In the case of a birth, the time allowed for registration is forty-two days. Registration could, therefore, have taken place in a quarter following the date of birth.

The district of registration is the local area registry or county registry and is not always the exact place of birth. It is as well to know the names of the surrounding towns and boroughs if you are researching a fairly common surname.

Information as to the maiden name of the mother is only required when ordering copy certificates for births registered after the September quarter of the year 1911.

A birth certificate as a starting point gives you a great deal of information. Armed with those details, you are on your way to a thrilling journey into the past. You can now start searching for the parents' marriage details in the GRO marriage indexes. Also if a census (see Chapter 7) took place near the date of the birth, you can use the information given on the birth certificate about the father's address to help you find the census returns for the family which may reveal details of other family members and their ages.

Death Certificates

A death certificate will give the following information:

1. Date and place of death.
2. Name and surname.
3. Sex.
4. Age at death.
5. Occupation.
6. Cause of death.
7. Name of informer.
8. Qualification of informer (relationship to deceased).
9. Date of registration.

Certificates issued for deaths after 1969 will also give the date and place of birth of the deceased, the maiden name of a woman if married and the usual address of the informant. In particular, the date and place of birth can be very helpful.

The indexes of the death registers can be searched in the same way as those for births. From 1865 the age at death is given in the index so that, if there are two people with the same name, the age at death can help to pinpoint the one you are looking for. If you know roughly how old the person was when they died and the age at death shown is many years different it is probably the wrong person.

A death certificate which includes the age of the deceased will, of course, help you to work out his or her date of birth. You can then search the GRO birth indexes for the birth records. If the deceased was a widow or widower, you can also start looking in the death indexes for the death of that spouse. As with birth certificates, any addresses given can be searched in the census.

Marriage Certificates

A marriage certificate will give you the following information:

1. Date.
2. Names and surnames of the bride and groom.
3. Ages of the bride and groom. (Sometimes a certificate will simply say 'full age' or 'minor'. 'Full age' means that the spouse was 21 or older; 'minor' means that the spouse was under 21.)
4. Descriptions (spinster, bachelor, etc.).
5. Professions.
6. Addresses.
7. Names of the fathers of both parties.
8. Occupations of both fathers.
9. Names of witnesses.

The marriage indexes are searched in a similar manner to the birth indexes. One advantage is that you can cross check that you have the correct marriage by looking in the same quarter under the names of both the bride and groom. If the volume and page numbers are the same for each, you have the correct marriage entry and can proceed to apply for a copy certificate.

If the marriage took place from 1984 onwards, no quarter is shown in the index. There is a column beside the names headed 'REG' and that reference should be entered on your application form instead of the quarter. ('REG' is an internal reference used by the Registry.)

If you are married, look for your own entry, if not, look for that of your parents. All you need to know are the names of the groom, the maiden name of the bride, the date and place of the marriage. The place is not quite so essential since if you have both names you can cross check that you have the correct entry and the index will give you the district of the registry.

If the marriage certificate includes the ages of the bride and groom, you should be able to search the birth indexes to find their birth details. However, be aware that brides and grooms often gave incorrect ages, particularly if the woman was older than the man at the time of the marriage. The addresses of the fathers given on the certificate may help you to find the parents in the nearest census to the wedding (see Chapter 7).

How to Obtain Certificates

You can order and pay for certificates online at the website of the General Register Office. The first time you use the site you will need to register by giving your name, postal and email addresses, and selecting a password. Once this is done, you simply enter your email address and chosen password each time you wish to order a certificate. Follow the instructions on screen and make sure you enter the correct details for the certificate you are ordering (such as volume and page number). One digit wrong and you will not get your certificate or you may get the wrong one – an expensive and time-consuming mistake. You can order a certificate for an event registered after 1900 without quoting its reference number but it is more expensive.

It is possible to buy copy certificates through other commercial websites, some even with the word 'gov' in their name. However, you should be aware that these sites are not the official GRO website but are the websites of commercial companies. As always when buying something online, make sure you know who you are dealing with and compare the prices on offer.

If you prefer not to purchase online, you can order copy certificates from the GRO by post or fax or telephone.

You can buy copy certificates from the register office which covers the area where the event was originally registered if you know the date (preferably the actual day, or at least the quarter and year), the parish or town where the event took place and the name(s) of the parties involved. Check the relevant local authority website for details of what is available, the cost and how to pay. The volume and page references which you need to order certificates from the General Register Office are usually not of use to a local register office so try to give as much other relevant information as possible to the Registrar (for example, names of both parents for a birth certificate; name of the particular church for a marriage certificate) so that the information you are seeking can be found as quickly as possible.

The more certificates you obtain, the more you will be able to evaluate the information they contain in relation to further research.

Adoptions

There were no official adoption certificates before 1920 and the Adopted Children Register shows all adoptions granted by the courts in England and Wales since 1927. It is very difficult to trace earlier records. When an adoption order is made by a court, a new birth entry is made in the Adopted Children Register which replaces the original entry. The Adopted Children Register is not open to public research.

Indexes for adoption certificates show only the adoptive names and the names of the adopting parents. They do not give the name of the person before adoption. They are similar to a normal birth certificate, except that the surname shown is not the name at birth. Some children were adopted by close relatives, in which case the surname could possibly be the same but the certificate would not reveal this.

Only an adult adopted person can obtain a copy of the original birth certificate showing the name of the natural parents. This might mean that you are unable to trace your family history through that line if you find that a parent or grandparent was adopted. A substantial amount of information is required in order to obtain such a certificate: the date of the adoption, the court where the order was made, the full names and surname of the adoptive parents and the name of the child (adoptive surname).

For adoptions up to and including 11 November 1975 adopted people wishing to see their original birth certificates are required to see and be counselled by a social worker before the information is made available to them. For adoptions after 12 November 1975 the adopted person has a choice whether to be counselled or not. Since 2005 birth relatives have been able to apply for access to the Register. Written application must be made.

Scotland and Northern Ireland have their own adoption procedures. Children born in England and Wales but adopted in Scotland, Ireland or overseas need to apply to the General Register Office.

For more information on adoption, see the website of the General Register Office.

3

BIRTH, MARRIAGE AND DEATH CERTIFICATES (ELSEWHERE IN THE UK, THE ISLE OF MAN AND THE CHANNEL ISLANDS)

Scotland

Family historians whose families have roots in Scotland have an advantage over those whose records are in England and Wales.

Scottish civil registration did not commence until 1 January 1855 but their record keeping was much more thorough than that of England and Wales. All the certificates of births, marriages and deaths contain more information than the English certificates.

Birth certificates give, in addition to the information on the English certificates, one important addition: the date and place of the parents' marriage. This enables the searcher to obtain a copy marriage certificate for the parents without having to search the indexes quarter by quarter, year by year from the date of the child's birth to find the marriage date. Marriage certificates give the names of both parents of the bride and the groom, not only that of the father as on their English counterparts. Death certificates give the names of both parents of the deceased. All this additional information is most helpful and saves a great deal of research time.

The first birth, death and marriage certificates, issued in 1855, contained much additional information. The birth certificates give the parents' ages and birthplaces and the number of other siblings living and deceased. The marriage certificates give the places of present residence and the usual residence if different of both bride and groom and details of any previous marriages. The death certificates give the place of birth, details of marriage, burial place and all living and deceased siblings. Sadly, for genealogists and family historians, as the volume of work grew, the inclusion of this additional information was not continued after 1855.

Scottish records are held in New Register House, Edinburgh (see Appendix). For an inclusive search fee the researcher has access to the indexes from 1855 for births, marriages and deaths, and divorces from May 1984. Also available are old parish registers from 1553 to 1855 and the census records from 1841 to 1901.

Each researcher is given a numbered seat at a desk. All indexes are on computer and searching is very easy. Instructions for use are given at each terminal and the computer will offer various recorded spellings for each name. There is also a very useful cross check for female marriages and deaths as these are indexed under all known surnames, i.e. maiden surname, previous and present married names.

Original records are not open for inspection but most are available on self service access microfiche or microfilm so you can check you have the correct entry before ordering and paying for copy certificates. You can also get photocopies, without purchasing certificates, for all old parish records, open census records (1841–1901), birth entries 100 years and older, marriage entries 75 years and older, and death entries 50 years and older. To protect the privacy of people still living you are not able to photocopy "modern entries" and must purchase an official certificate if you wish to take these entries away with you. However, you are free to make your own notes from the image on the screen if you prefer. (Remember to cite your sources!)

One visit at New Register House could help you uncover several generations. If you find a correct birth certificate this will give you the names and ages of both parents; a marriage certificate will give you the names of both sets of parents. Note this information and return to the indexes to search for the relevant page and volume numbers.

When you have found your entry in the computer index, complete the relevant (colour coded) order form. Take the microfiche or microfilm that you require and replace it with your order form, first detaching the counterfoil on which you should have noted the entry number that you wish to search. You can remove three fiches or two films at a time. After use, put them in the relevant trays for filing. If you require some minor records, fill in an orange order form and put it in a request tray. An attendant will bring the register to your seat number.

The attendants are very knowledgeable; they can often point you in the right direction if the record inspected proves to be the wrong one and will help you to master the equipment.

Before visiting New Register House it is advisable to book your seat in advance by letter, email or phone. The Registry issue very informative free literature (which can be obtained by post or accessed on their website) showing what records they hold, their charges and times of opening, which will help you plan your visit in advance. There are, of course, charges for copy certificates; these are less if you search the indexes yourself but you may find that the assistance of the Registry staff is worth the extra charge. You may only use pencils here; they sell them in aid of a local charity to anyone who forgets to bring one.

If you are unable to visit Edinburgh yourself, you might like to search the index of Scottish birth, death and marriage records now available on the ScotlandsPeople website which is run by the General Register Office for Scotland and the National Archives of Scotland in partnership with a web publisher called Scotland on Line. To respect the privacy of people living, internet access to the actual records has been restricted to birth records over 100 years old, marriage records over 75 years old and death records over 100 years old, but you can order an extract (an officially certified copy of the register entry) of these records to be posted to you.

There is a genealogy centre in Glasgow with computer terminals giving access to the national index in Edinburgh (see Appendix). You will need to book early by telephoning the centre in order to reserve a place. A daily search fee is charged. There is good access for disabled users.

Ireland

Civil registration in Ireland commenced on 1 January 1864.

Birth certificates in Ireland give the date and exact place of birth, the name of the child, the full name, occupation and residence of the father, the maiden name of the mother and the name of the person present at the birth.

Marriage certificates give the names of the parties, date and place of the marriage, the place of residence of the bride and groom and the names of their fathers.

Death certificates only give the name of the deceased, the age and the date and place of death.

The General Register Office maintains a genealogical research room in Dublin (see the Appendix for details) where you can search the indexes to the birth, death and marriage records and obtain photocopies of records identified from the indexes.

You can also order copies of certificates by post and fax

and in person from the General Register Office in Roscommon. Application forms can be downloaded from the GRO's website and payment can be made by credit card.

Northern Ireland

All the original registers and records for Northern Ireland which commence with the partition of Ireland in 1922 are kept in the General Register Office, Belfast (see Appendix). The Belfast registry also holds some records for the northern counties of southern Ireland (the counties of Cavan, Monaghan and Donegal). This is because before partition these counties were part of Ulster.

Birth certificates will give you the date and place of birth, name, sex; full name, occupation and usual residence of father; maiden name of mother; date of registration and name and residence of informant.

Marriage certificates give the date, names and ages of both bride and groom together with their residences at the date of marriage and their occupations, the names of the fathers of the bride and groom and their occupations.

Information on death certificates is similar to that given on English certificates.

The Belfast General Register Office has a unique system to assist family history researchers. It offers them the choice of two types of search: an assisted search and an index search. An assisted search involves a general search of the records with the assistance of the office staff for any period of years and any number of entries. This is naturally quite expensive and there is usually a waiting list for this service. You may need to book some time in advance.

With an index search, you search the indexes yourself but then the staff are able to check up to four of the entries you have made. You can then pay extra if you need further verification.

You can also order copy certificates by post, by telephone and by fax. At the time of writing, the internet service is being redeveloped so check their website for the latest details.

The Isle of Man

Here again, if your family originally came from the Isle of Man and, even if they moved on around the world which many Manxmen did, all the records are held in close proximity. Compulsory registration commenced in 1878, and all the research can be carried out at the Registry, which is on the ground floor of the General Registry building in Douglas (see Appendix). The information available from the certificates is similar to that shown in certificates from England and Wales. There are no search fees and the indexes are on microfiche. For a small fee you can see the original registers once you have found the entries you require. Copies of the certificates are obtainable on payment of a fee.

The Channel Islands

Civil registration of births, marriages and deaths began in Jersey in August 1842. Copies of these registers from this date are held by the Superintendent Registrar on the island (see Appendix). No copies are available in the UK. The copies are kept by parish and there is no all-island index. However, the public can look through the files containing the indexes at the Superintendent Registrar's office or can ask for certificates to be sent to them by post or can ask for a search to be made on their behalf. Fees, of course, are applicable in both instances. Indexes to these registers are also available at the library of the Société Jersiaise (see Appendix) and at the Jersey Archive (see Appendix).

Civil registration of births, marriages and deaths began in Guernsey in 1840. It included the islands of Herm and Jethou.

Central registration in Guernsey of events in Sark and Alderney began in 1925. Each register is indexed on an island-wide basis except for deaths before 1963 which are indexed parish by parish. Searches of the indexes, which are held at the Greffe in St Peter Port, may be conducted in person or certificates may be obtained from the Registrar General there (see Appendix). Duplicates of the nineteenth century Greffe birth, marriage and death records are held at the Priaulx Library (see Appendix).

All the registries will supply copy certificates by mail provided you can give them sufficient information and send the correct fee with your application. In the case of birth certificates they require the full name of the person, the date and place of birth and the name of the parents. The maiden name of the mother is only required for entries after September 1911. For marriage certificates, the date and place, full names of both parties and the names of the fathers if possible. For death certificates, the full name of the deceased, place and date of death. If the person was married, the full name of the spouse is also helpful. Charges vary from registry to registry. A telephone call direct to the registry in question will elicit their requirements as to fees and save time and correspondence.

Most registries do not have the facilities for protracted correspondence and are unable to deal with detailed written enquiries. If incorrect applications are made, they will be returned with a printed form stating what is wrong, usually by the method of ticking the various printed options.

4

KEEPING YOUR RECORDS

What is the main objective of the family historian? It is exactly the same as that of the professional historian: to record the historical events and genealogy of a family, offering the reader a well documented presentation, interesting not only to the historian and his family but to anyone who chooses to read it.

Record keeping is sometimes felt to be the most difficult area of family history research. Family trees often have gaps and no cross references so that clear identification of individual members of the family and their relationships is not possible. Careful methodical recording not only helps you to clarify and direct your own thoughts, but can act as a guide showing where to commence your next searches. It is also an important requisite if your researches are to be of assistance to future researchers. It is important to record both negative and positive searches so that you can remember where you were *unable* to find some piece of information and do not duplicate the work. It also gives direction if you stop at any given point and do not follow up the result of a piece of research. You will know that there is material there to follow up later.

Now that you have amassed a fair amount of material, the time has come to decide how you will store and record it and how you should prepare your first family tree. If you have

never worked in an office, where filing and collating information are routine, don't be daunted by what may seem to you an
endless amount of paperwork. While you are recording and
sorting all the information you have collected it will begin to
fall into some sort of order and you will understand what you
are trying to do.

The main points to bear in mind are that you wish to achieve:

1. The recording of all the information gained, in a system
   giving easy access to that information.
2. The safe storage of original documents in a system easily
   displayed.
3. The preparation of a simple, easily followed family tree.

Computer Records
A computer can be a great help in keeping and collating your
records – you can store a large amount of information and
back it up onto just one or two disks. Data can be recorded on
CD, DVD or USB flash drives. New devices are certain to
appear on the market and you will have to decide which is best
for your purpose.

It is possible to buy specially written genealogical programs
on disks or CDs for your PC or Mac on which you can store your
family records. At the time of writing, popular software for PC
owners includes *Family Tree Maker*, *Roots Magic*, *Family
Historian* and *Legacy*, while Mac users can use *Reunion* and
Heredis.

These programs are frequently updated and very comprehensive. They will enable you to prepare and print family
trees and charts. They will collate family relationships, ages,
birth and death dates, and index source material. You can
usually scan in photographs. Most programs will also question
any entries you make that do not agree with each other and
will draw your attention to dates and relationships if you

appear to get them wrong. This is particularly helpful if your family used the same first name for the first male of several generations. If you have several 'Williams' born over a period of 100 years, the computer program will question you if you enter the dates or relationships incorrectly.

Another benefit of using specialized genealogy software is that most family history computer programs provide the facility of creating a GEDCOM file of your family tree. This is an easy way to share information with others researching the same family. You can either email your GEDCOM file to fellow researchers or upload it directly to a website. Others can also send you their GEDCOM files which you can 'import' into your own computer program.

Some of the genealogical software is quite costly so it is essential to purchase the program that suits your require- ments and is the easiest for you to use. Many manufacturers produce updates for their programs which add to the cost if you wish to keep up to date. To get the very latest on what each computer program offers, carry out a search on the internet and read the computer articles in family history magazines.

A good method of viewing these programs is to visit a family history fair where such items are exhibited and where you may be allowed a 'hands on' try with the programs. Beware if you are not an experienced computer user: the demonstrators are trained to make everything look very easy and you may find it difficult once you are on your own at home. Most manufacturers do, however, offer a support telephone number which you can ring for assistance if necessary.

An alternative to buying a complete computer program is to purchase what are known as 'Shareware' disks. These give limited access to programs at a much reduced cost. There are companies specializing in the supply of genealogy programs and Shareware disks (see the Appendix). They also supply data CDs containing parish records and census extracts which can be very useful. Before purchasing data CDs, make sure they contain the information you require and will use frequently.

If you do not wish to go to the expense of buying a special genealogical program you can, of course, set up your own system for storing information on your computer, in a similar way to storing manual records. For details of a *very basic* method of maintaining records on your computer, see page 48.

Manual Records

Alternatively, if you prefer, you can keep your records manually. The following are some suggestions.

A visit to any office stationer or a search on the internet will give you some idea of the many methods of storage and information recording now available: rigid plastic boxes and card index cabinets, folders, box, concertina and pocket files, plastic document holders and display envelopes, loose flat files and photograph albums. The possibilities are many and varied. The cost varies widely also, therefore a great deal should not be spent until you discover the method which you find easiest and which will fit into the space you have available.

Recording the Information

How are you going to keep your records? Chronologically (date order) or by name? The answer is both, by using a system of cross references. The easiest method is to use a card index system which can also be colour coded, using the same colour cards for each family which will make it even easier for quick access. For your main family (probably your father's surname) the cards can be white; for your next family (probably your mother's family surname) the cards can be blue. You can use any colour combination you choose. If you prefer to use only one colour of card you can use a system with coloured marking pens, highlighting connecting members of one family by drawing a line through the names, using a different colour for each family.

Cards, ruled or plain, together with plain and indexed guide cards in various colours to be inserted between the groups can be purchased in several sizes and you will soon discover the best size for you. Rigid plastic boxes with hinged lids, which hold approximately 1,000 cards, to fit the various sizes of cards are readily available, as are larger index cabinets with movable divisions. If you are going to adopt the card colour coding system, a card box for each colour might prove the best method with which to begin. If you are using the marker system, one large cabinet with colour coded divisions could be used. It is essential that all boxes and files be clearly labelled showing the contents.

If you do not wish to commit yourself to a particular card size when you first start your records, clear plastic food boxes with different coloured lids in many sizes are available and are less expensive than the custom made boxes. They can be used quite effectively to store your card index system. Even more economical is the use of strong cardboard boxes with lids. If you wonder why I emphasize that your storage boxes should have lids, the reason is that paper seems to gather dust wherever it is stored. While over the years your cards may look a little dog-eared from constant usage, if they are kept in covered containers they will keep cleaner and will not have to be renewed so often.

As you sort, evaluate and record the information you have gathered, you will need somewhere to keep the original notes you have made. These can be kept in box files, one box to each family, the notes kept in either alphabetically indexed sections or simply in chronological order inside the box. Alternatively, they can be kept in concertina files or individual pocket or wallet files. The pocket or wallet files which can be purchased in different colours to match your colour codes and are reasonably priced may be the best when starting.

When you have decided on the card size and method you are going to use, as an exercise, start with yourself and record all the information that you have. In order to save time and space, there are standard genealogical abbreviations for frequently used words which are used universally as follows:

b.	born	*div.*	divorced
bapt.	baptised	*dau.*	daughter
bur.	buried	*unm.*	unmarried
d.	died	=	married
m.	male	*f.*	female

Two other words frequently used in genealogy are 'spouse' meaning marriage partner either male or female and 'siblings' meaning brothers and sisters in the same family.

Always write the date in full; do not use abbreviations or numbers for the months. Abbreviations for January, June and July (Jan., Jun., Jul.) can be confusing, and September has not always been the ninth month. Dates should be recorded with the day first, followed by the month and the year – 27 January 1899.

Using your white cards, or whatever colour you have chosen for your family name, begin by recording the name cards with the following information on one card:

Top line:	capital letters	your name
Second line:	b. (for born)	date of birth
Third line:	at	place of birth
Fourth line:	married	date of marriage
Fifth line:	at	place of marriage
Sixth line:	father	name of father
Seventh line:	mother	maiden name of mother

If you are unmarried put 'unm' beside your name and don't

include the lines referring to the date and place of marriage. If you are married, continue:

| Eighth line: | spouse | name of husband/wife |
| Ninth line: | children | names and sex of children |

Beside your name in the top right hand corner of the card put your reference number 'W1' (1 for the first name to be recorded and 'W' for white). If you use only white cards your reference should show the colour of marker used for each family, i.e. R1 (red), B1 (blue), G1 (green), etc. If you have family names that you intend to follow at a later date you could give them the reference 'M' for miscellaneous and need not give them a colour. Additional information such as when and where baptised can be included on the back of the card. You can also record a note of where your copy birth certificate and any other documents are held. It may be necessary, as you gather more information, to use more than one card for each person, but provided you use your reference numbers and file all the cards for one person together this will prove no problem.

From this information you can prepare more white cards.

Top line:	capital letters	his full name	'W2'
Second line:	b. (for born)	date of birth	
Third line:	at	place of birth	
Fourth line:	married	date of marriage	
Fifth line:	at	place of marriage	
Sixth line:	father	father's full name	
Seventh line:	mother	mother's name	
Eighth line:	spouse	maiden name of wife	
Ninth line:	children	names and sex of children	

Your own name as connecting link will appear on the ninth

SMITH, LESLIE GEORGE   W1

b.	1 January 1923
at	County Borough of West Ham
married	27 March 1949
at	County Borough of West Ham
father	SMITH, CHARLES WILLIAM (W2)
mother	ROBERTS, JEANNIE REBECCA (R1)
spouse	CARTER, ESTHER (B1)
children	Anthony (W13), Susan (W14)

(a)

Occupation – Link Man, Royal Opera House,
        Covent Garden

Served British Navy (Chief Petty Officer)
        1940 – 1945

Birth & Marriage Certificates, Navy Discharge
        Papers, Photographs (Book 2)

(b)

Fig. 2.   (a) Front of index card for Leslie George Smith.
            (b) Back of index card for Leslie George Smith.

line and you can put the number 'W1' beside it to show where further information can be obtained concerning yourself.

As you proceed making and numbering cards you can put the references beside all the connecting names. Put as much information as you have on each card. Update the cards when more information comes to light. As you go further back in time, you might enter on the back of the cards a note of where the information was obtained. It is essential to cite your sources of information, as emphasized in previous chapters. When you have had some practice of record making you will

SMITH, GEORGE WILLIAM JOSEPH   W3

b.	23 April 1878
at	Dartford, Kent
married	19 November 1898
at	Dartford, Kent
d.	25 December 1939
at	Dartford
father	SMITH, WILLIAM CHARLES (W4)
mother	DEAN, SARAH ANN (M6)
spouse	SHARPE, EMMA JANE (M5)
children	Susan (W7), Eliza (W8), Charles William (W2), Ann Sophia Dean (W9)

(a)

Occupation – Journeyman

Lived Mount Pleasant House, Dartford,
    Kent all his life

Bapt. St. Mark's Church, Dartford, Kent

Birth, Death & Marriage Certificates
    (Book 1)

(b)

Fig. 3.   (a) Back of index card for George William Joseph Smith.
            (b) Front of index card for George William Joseph Smith.

be able to decide what information you wish to include on each card, but a general rule is to record as much as you know about each person. Cards should be kept for each individual encountered.

Figs. 2 and 3 are a set of name cards for my own family which I started many years ago as a beginner, only the surnames are changed. I have remained faithful to this system of recording which helps me to find all available information quickly. From these samples you will see how the reference numbers at the top of each card appear on other cards so that you will have easy access to any person by referring to the numbers and finding the cards. You will also see the reason for numbering each person recorded. In many families male children are named after fathers or grandfathers and female children after grandmothers or favourite aunts. Some families have a tradition of giving the firstborn son the same name through the generations and Scots families sometimes give a son his mother's family name as first name. So, unless there is a clear identification of each name, the records could soon become muddled and difficult to follow.

If you are using a separate box for each family, the cards can be filed numerically, using the reference numbers. Alternatively if you are using one box for all your cards you can file the cards alphabetically by surname. As a cross reference a set of cards can be prepared on a chronological basis, filed in date order. These will not require reference numbers, but will, of course, show the reference numbers of each person beside the names. Samples of these cards are given in Fig. 4.

These index cards are for your own use and will form the basis of the information shown on your family trees and in your written history. If you are asked how you know that a distant relative was deported to Australia for stealing a loaf of bread, your index cards will tell you where you obtained the information and where any documentation is stored.

It is important at this stage to start a general information and address book or card index. The book can be a loose-leaf ring binder with two sections, one divided alphabetically for addresses. Or you can continue to use a card index system. Enter in alphabetical order every address you need and even those you think you may not need again: relatives, registries, record offices and archives, bookshops, family history

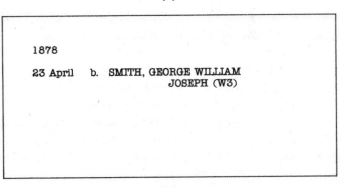

```
1922

24 June    Married

           SMITH, CHARLES WILLIAM (W2)
           ROBERTS, JEANNIE REBECCA (R1)
```

(a)

```
1878

23 April   b.  SMITH, GEORGE WILLIAM
                     JOSEPH (W3)
```

(b)

Fig. 4.   (a)   Chronological index card for 1922.
       (b)   Chronological index card for 1878.

societies, parish councils and cemeteries. I recently received a letter from an unknown person in Australia seeking my help in tracing a document. He had been given my address by someone I met at a genealogical conference many months ago. My address, taken by someone I would probably never meet again, had proved useful to her. Genealogists and family historians are inveterate note takers, hoarding any snippets of information like squirrels hoarding nuts for the winter!

Any other information such as opening times of libraries, the cost of documents, where to buy certain items, can be entered in the general information section. You will soon learn to distinguish what sort of information will be helpful and which you wish to record.

At this stage of preparing your family history patience and meticulous attention to detail are required. If record making appears a tedious exercise at first, persevere. It will soon become second nature and you will enjoy completing your cards, adding information as it is obtained. Your diligence will also be rewarded when after several years' work you are still able to return to your first notes and find information without difficulty.

Simple Computer Record-Keeping

In your word processing program create a new document to store the information you want to keep on yourself. Give the document a name, for example, your surname followed by your first names. Then enter the same information that you would enter if you were maintaining manual records, in particular include your relationship to other family members, using the letter and number references. The information on both sides of the cards in Figs. 2 and 3 can be stored on just one page of your computer document, as shown in Figs. 7 and 8. Once you have entered and saved all the information on yourself, close that document and create a new one for each other member of your family you are researching. In every case, name the document by using the appropriate surname and first names. This means that, when you open the relevant file or folder where the documents are stored, the computer should list them in alphabetical order, making it easy for you to find the correct document.

You can also make a chronological index on the computer. Simply create a new document for each year and enter the relevant information in it. Again, when you open the relevant file or folder, the computer will list them in ascending order so you'll easily be able to open the appropriate document to add new facts.

A document containing general information can also be created. You may find it useful to print out a copy of this and store it, so that you can have access to the details in it without having to use your computer every time.

When using a computer to store information, make sure you *always* back up your files onto a separate disk or device. It would be a catastrophe if you "lost" your records because of a computer failure.

Storing Original Documents

Copy birth, death and marriage certificates, original letters, photocopies, photographs and precious elderly papers need to be stored so that they do not suffer damage but can be easily displayed for they will play a major supporting role when you show your family history. Once again a visit to a stationery suppliers or a search on the internet will enable you to evaluate the various methods available. Books of clear acid-free plastic pockets are available in many sizes and with a range in the number of pockets they contain. The covers, usually with an outside pocket for a label, come in several colours and can be used to fit in with your colour coding. Where documents such as certificates need to be read on only one side, two can be placed back to back in one pocket. Letters, if written on two sides of a page, can easily be read. The plastic pockets can be turned like the pages of a book and will protect the documents. An index of contents can be placed in a pocket provided on the inside cover or in the first pocket if preferred. These documents can be filed chronologically, starting with the present day and working backwards or with the earliest documents you have and working forwards to the present day. (See Figs. 5 and 6.)

For each person you may have a birth, marriage and death certificate, a baptismal certificate and several other documents such as a photocopy of a Bible entry, or newspaper items

CONTENTS

1. Fragments of history – The Smith Family (author unknown)
2. Handwritten Parliamentary Return – Smith family with initialled note "DS 1815"
3. Memorandum handwritten by William Charles Smith 1867 with handwritten family history
4. Receipt 1900 – William Charles Smith
5. Letter 1878 – Sarah Ann Dean
6. Copy Memorandum – handwritten by William Smith
7. Extract from Charles William Smith's Manuscript Book
8. Handwritten note re Smith of Dartford (author unknown)
9. Smith family tree – letter E. Smith (undated)
10. Handwritten notes re Smith family (author unknown)
11. Handwritten Smith Family Tree (author unknown)
12. Letter 1894 – Jessie Smith
13. Letter 1894 – Rev. R. S. Graves
14. Smith place names with note Rev. R. S. Graves
15. Handwritten note re Smith family (author unknown)
16. Handwritten note re Smith family 1907
17. Letter 1912 – Frederick Appleton
18. Handwritten copy of The Parish Registers of Dartford made by Charles Smith of Barringdon Street
19. Letter Margaret F. Smith
20. Drawing Smith family crest (artist unknown)

Fig. 5. Example contents page for plastic pockets.

CONTENTS

1. Census Return – Dartford District 1851.
2. Census Record – West Ham 1871.
3. Marriage Certificate – William Charles Smith (W4)/Sarah Ann Dean (M6)
4. Death Certificate – William Charles Smith (W4)
5. Copy Will and Grant of Probate – William Charles Smith (W4)
6. Birth Certificate – Samuel Charles Smith (W5)
7. Death Certificate – Samuel Charles Smith (W5)
8. Marriage Certificate – George William Joseph Smith (W3)/Emma Jane Sharpe (M5)
9. Copy Will and Grant of Probate – George William Joseph Smith (W3)
10. Copy Will and Grant of Probate – Emma Jane Smith née Sharpe (M5)
11. Marriage Certificate – William Smith (W6)/Ann Perkins (M8)
12. Marriage Certificate – George Henry Roberts (R2)/Sarah Jane Dowsett (M1)
13. Birth Certificate – Charles William Smith (W2)
14. Photographs – 6 Constance Street, Silvertown, West Ham (W2)
15. Photographs – Mount Pleasant House, Dartford (W3)
16. Photograph – Wedding: Charles William Smith (W2)/Jeannie Rebecca Roberts (R1)
17. Photographs – Burial plot showing memorial column and enclosure rails, Highgate Cemetery: Samuel Charles Smith (W5), George William Joseph Smith (W3), Emma Jane Smith née Sharpe (M5), Susan Smith (W7) and Eliza Smith (W8)
18. Map and booklet – Highgate Cemetery
19. Photocopy – pages 'Past and Present' relating to West Ham

Fig. 6.   Example contents page.
This one shows cross-references to index cards.

referring to a 21st birthday celebration, giving the names of those present (very useful if you are able to make the family connections). Keep all the documents relating to one person together placing them in the pockets in chronological order, thus building a picture of his or her life and times. It is these certificates and documents which will put the meat on the bones of your family history and bring the people to life. The reference numbers and colour codes can be used in the index to link the documentation with the information cards. Figs. 5 and 6 are sample index/contents pages showing the documents which can be displayed. The information where the documents are stored can be entered on the index cards as a cross reference.

Photographs can be kept in conventional photograph albums or in an album with loose-leaf pages each with its own clear acid-free plastic cover. The photographs are placed on the stiff pages under the covers and are easily moved and changed round. Each photograph should be clearly identified. If of a person, the individual should be named and their reference number shown. If a photograph of a house or a monumental inscription, details should be given and a reference number of the person to whom the picture relates. Photographs can be kept in the folders with other information if preferred. A plastic pocket will hold several photographs. Details can be written on a piece of card inserted in the pocket. A small piece of double-sided sticky tape or a tiny spot of 'Blu-tack' will hold the pictures in position, but they will be movable when required. If a card slightly smaller in size than the pocket is used this will give support to flimsy photographs. Photographs and information can be placed on each side of the card, making the most economic use of a plastic pocket.

One company that specializes in storage supplies is Genealogical Storage. (See Appendix.)

SMITH, LESLIE GEORGE

Born	1 January 1923
At	County Borough of West Ham
Married	27 March 1949
At	County Borough of West Ham
Father	SMITH, CHARLES WILLIAM (W2)
Mother	ROBERTS, JEANNIE REBECCA (R1)
Spouse	CARTER, ESTHER (B1)
Children	Anthony (W13)
	Susan (W14)
Occupation	Link Man, Royal Opera House, Covent Garden
	Served British Navy (Chief Petty Officer) 1940-1945

Documents held

Birth and marriage certificates, Navy discharge papers, photographs (Book 2)

Fig. 7. Computer record showing information held on Leslie George Smith.

SMITH, GEORGE WILLIAM JOSEPH

Born	23 April 1878
At	Dartford, Kent
Married	19 November 1898
At	Dartford, Kent
Died	25 December 1939
At	Dartford
Father	SMITH, WILLIAM CHARLES (W4)
Mother	DEAN, SARAH ANN (M6)
Spouse	SHARPE, EMMA JANE (M5)
Children	Susan (W7)
	Eliza (W8)
	Charles William (W2)
	Ann Sophia Dean (W9)
Occupation	Journeyman
Lived at	Mount Pleasant House, Dartford, Kent all his life
Bapt at	St Mark's Church, Dartford, Kent

Documents held
Birth, death and marriage certificates (Book 1)

Fig. 8. Computer record showing information held on George William Joseph Smith.

5

YOUR FIRST FAMILY TREE

If you are using a computer program, the program will prepare a family tree from the information you have entered. Most programs will produce both descendant and ascendant trees. Fig. 9 shows an ancestor tree produced by *Family Tree Maker*, a computer program available on CD Rom. You can decide how many generations you wish to show in your family tree and enter this instruction in the program. You may also have the option to show siblings and relationships on your chart.

Several genealogical websites, including Find My Past and Ancestry, now provide free programs which will build a family tree for you.

If you prefer to draw your family tree on paper yourself, this gives you more flexibility since the size and style are up to you. However, preparing and drawing your first family tree by hand from the information you have gathered requires patience and experimentation. It will probably be necessary to try several drafts before deciding on the size, style and shape you wish to adopt. The amount of detail recorded will be up to you and will depend upon the depth of your researches, but a simple family tree will be helpful and will encourage you to go on with the work.

It is rare for a family tree to be complete in every detail; too many individuals appear without full information. Relation-

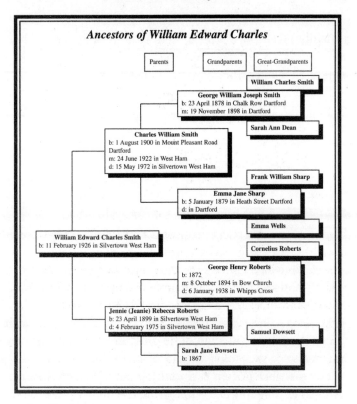

Fig. 9. An ancestor tree produced by Family Tree Maker.

ships are not always clearly defined, but if your tree is based upon the information contained in your card or computer index, with the reference numbers shown by each name, missing information can be checked from time to time and when obtained added to the chart and the card or computer. It is important to include the reference numbers since if you prepare a chart for each family name you will then have a cross reference to show where the family relationships lie between the families by referring to the numbers given to each person.

It is impossible even to contemplate recording every name on a single chart. I have known a researcher use a roll of wallpaper, but even that gave insufficient room and was very difficult to read since it meant rolling it up from one end until the name required was reached and the rolled ends kept snapping together if they were not held strongly apart.

How and where you store the charts will play a part in deciding the size. They can be stored flat in a drawer or rolled and held by elastic bands. Rolling the charts gives more storage room, but makes it necessary to pin them out on a board for easy reading. A chart for each family could be prepared on size A3 (16½" × 11¾"/420mm × 297mm) paper and a display book with plastic pockets used. The charts could then be placed back to back with thin card between to support them, two in each pocket so that a book of 20 pockets could hold 40 charts. The charts could be shown chronologically commencing either with the earliest known name or your own name. The final family tree (following only your paternal line) might be framed and hung in a prominent position in your house. It could be handwritten for you by a calligrapher in special lettering with names in different colours and line drawings of associated houses or places.

It is possible to purchase printed family charts in many sizes, some fanciful and some plain, coloured or black and white. The Society of Genealogists offers a choice of several as does the Federation of Family History Societies. Genealogical magazines contain advertisements for many different styles of chart: a chart with a printed tree – usually an oak – with the main family name on the trunk of the tree and spaces for names on the branches; a large circle with a space in the middle for the main name and segments for each family radiating outwards. The choices are many and varied as is the cost. If you join your local family history society or visit the Society of Genealogists you will, no doubt, see the charts prepared by other members which may help you to decide on your final size and design.

Your first family tree or chart should, however, be a simple record of your findings, using the abbreviations given previously and should concentrate on one family only. As you progress, further charts can be prepared for each family with the reference numbers showing the links between the families. It is easiest at this stage to start with the present day and work back into the past although you may elect in your final chart to start with the first known person of the family and work forwards to the present day.

A reasonable size sheet on which to draft your first chart is A3 paper. This should give you ample room to display four generations. Lay the paper in front of you with the longest side at the top and the shorter side running vertically from top to bottom. Arm yourself with pencils, a 12" (30cm) rule and an eraser. It is preferable not to use biro or permanent ink when first drafting your chart. It is easy to go over the pencil work with ink when you are satisfied with your first efforts. Before starting, rough in the blocks where you think the names will come on the paper in order not to waste too many sheets on your drafts.

The following measurements are based on using A3 paper. Begin by blocking in the areas where the information is to be written. Against the left side of the paper, 5" (127mm) down from the top draw a horizontal line 3½" (89mm) long. Two inches (50mm) below that draw another horizontal line 3½" (89mm) long. Against the right hand edge of these lines, 3½" (89mm) down from the top of the page draw a vertical line 5" (127mm) long with horizontal lines of 3½" (89mm) each at the top and bottom. This will give three areas where your own name and those of your parents will be written. Follow across the page in a similar manner, dividing each area created by two. When you reach the right hand side of the page you will have four blocks marked out down the page. As you need more blocks, they will become smaller. Keep the horizontal lines at the same length of 3½" (89mm) all the way across the page but reduce the vertical lines first to 3" (76mm)

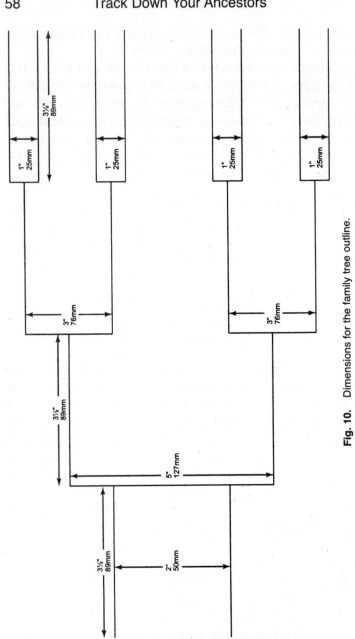

Fig. 10. Dimensions for the family tree outline.

and then to 1" (25mm). Fig. 10 shows how your page will look and gives the measurements of the lines.

Begin at the left hand side of the paper in the middle. Write in your name, with your reference number in brackets beside it, above the first horizontal line and the details from your card immediately under the line. If you are married write the name of your husband/wife on the second horizontal line with the details underneath the line. The following samples follow the index card examples shown in Chapter 4.

> SMITH, LESLIE GEORGE (W1)
> b.: 1 January 1923
> at: County Borough of West Ham
> married: 24 March 1949
> at: County Borough of West Ham
>
> CARTER, ESTHER (B1)
> b.: 2 November 1927
> at: London Borough of Hackney

You will require space for six lines under your own name and under each of the names of your father, grandfather and great-grandfather since this is the family name you are following. You will require space for four lines of information beneath the other names. Move across the page to the right and put your father's name on the next top horizontal line with his details under that line. Move down the page to the next horizontal line and put in your mother's name with her details under the line.

> SMITH, CHARLES WILLIAM (W2)
> b.: 1 August 1900
> at: Dartford, Kent
> father married: 24 June 1922
> at: West Ham, Essex
> d.: 15 May 1972
> at: London Borough of Newham

ROBERTS, JEANNIE REBECCA (R1)
b.: 23 April 1899
mother   at: County Borough of West Ham
d.: 4 February 1975
at: London Borough of Newham

Now you have two generations of your paternal line on paper, follow through across the page using the same method of horizontal and vertical lines to guide you. Add the third generation, your grandparents, and the fourth generation, your great-grandparents. The second main line will show your maternal grandparents and great-grandparents.

If you have roughed out the blocks first you should find the measurements given fit the paper size. If you use different sized paper you may find that you have left insufficient room to accommodate all the names and need to start several drafts until you reach a satisfactory result. Fig. 11 shows how your chart should look, with the names, references and details clearly shown. If there is information missing, you can put a question mark to denote that fact. If you wish to remind yourself of missing information that is to be researched you can mark the space with a small coloured sticky spot which can be removed when the information is inserted. These coloured spots can be purchased in packets in most stationers. In order to avoid confusion, I usually use small gold spots, a colour different from any of my family reference colours.

Looking at the chart you will see that although you wish to keep the chart to one family name, other names have been included, but the main family name being followed is always at the top of the page. You can then prepare similar charts using the same method for any other families researched. Although you will probably concentrate on one name when you start, information about other connected families will be gathered so that family charts can be started for each connecting family and completed as the information comes to light. Probably the next chart will concentrate on your mother's family name. Once started, most family researchers do not concentrate solely on their paternal line, nor try to research all their ancestors, but follow a few of the families as the intertwining details are gathered.

Turning to the sample chart in Fig. 11 you will see that you can learn quite a lot of information about the male lines of the Smith and Roberts families, that three generations of Smiths were born in Dartford in Kent and the Roberts family originated in Ireland, where they married and died, but little about their spouses and nothing about any other siblings.

If you wish to prepare a chart showing more detail of one family only, it is necessary to commence with the oldest known name. If you use this method, brothers and sisters, not shown, on the previous chart can be shown. Using the same size sheet of paper – A3 – start by putting the name in the centre at the top of the page. The following chart can be prepared commencing with the great-grandfather shown as the last entry on the previous chart. Write in the name and details as follows:

SMITH, WILLIAM   =   DEAN, SARAH ANN(M6)
CHARLES (W4)
1847–1907   1850–1900

Draw a short vertical line from the middle under the equals (married) sign then a horizontal line at the bottom of the vertical line. You can then show all the children of William Charles and Sarah Ann Dean by drawing short vertical lines down from the horizontal line and inserting their names, dates of birth and death, starting with the eldest on the left hand side. If they married you can also show the names of their partners. Fig. 12 shows a grid without the names but with the relationships. Follow the male lines which will always have the same family name. The children shown on the second horizontal line will be the second generation and those on the

SMITH, CHARLES WILLIAM (W2)

b.: 1 August 1900
at: Dartford, Kent
married: 24 June 1922
at: West Ham, Essex
d.: 15 May 1972
at: London Borough of Newham

SMITH, LESLIE GEORGE (W1)

b.: 1 January 1923
at: County Borough of West Ham
married: 27 March 1949
at: County Borough of West Ham

CARTER, ESTHER (B1)

b.: 2 November 1927
at: London Borough of Hackney

ROBERTS,
JEANNIE REBECCA (R1)

b.: 23 April 1899
at: County Borough of West Ham
d.: 4 February 1975
at: London Borough of Newham

Fig. 11.   Sample family tree.

SMITH, GEORGE WILLIAM JOSEPH (W3)

b.: 23 April 1878
at: Dartford, Kent
married: 19 November 1898
at: Dartford
d.: 25 December 1939
at: Dartford

SMITH, WILLIAM CHARLES (W4)

b.: 1847
at: Dartford, Kent
married: 27 May 1876
at: Dartford, Kent
d.: 8 July 1907
at: Dartford

DEAN, SARAH ANN (M6)

b.: 1850
at: Calcutta, India
d.: 1900

SHARPE, EMMA JANE (M5)

b.: 5 January 1879
at: Dartford, Kent
d.: 21 August 1950
at: Dartford

SHARPE, FRANK WILLIAM (M7)

b.: 1830
at: Dartford, Kent
married: ?
at: ?
d.: ?
at: ?

ROBERTS, GEORGE HENRY (R2)

b.: 17 October 1872
at: Co. Clare, Ireland
married: 8 October 1894
at: Bow Common, London
d.: 6 January 1938
at: Leyton, Essex

ROBERTS, CORNELIUS (R3)

b.: 1847
at: Ireland
married: ?
at: ?
d.: ?

BROWN, ELIZABETH (M4)

b.: 1846
at: West Ham, Essex
d.: ?

DOWSETT, SARAH JANE (M1)

b.: 9 September 1867
at: Braintree, Essex
d.: ?

DOWSETT, SAMUEL (M2)

b.: 1838
at: Halstead, Essex
married: 29 June 1860
at: Braintree, Essex
d.: 1 October 1878
at: Halstead

third horizontal line will be the third generation. Brothers and sisters of each generation will be shown and their children will be cousins. The names on the fourth generation will be the great grandchildren of the first name at the top of the page. Details of the female line may be entered, but not followed if there is insufficient room on the page. If you wish you can highlight your own line through the chart by using a different colour to write the names and the actual lines drawn from one generation to the next. It is quite difficult to plan this style of family tree to fit the space available, particularly if you wish to show as many of the family as possible. This could include brothers, sisters, uncles, aunts and cousins all belonging to the same family and is a chart which concentrates more particularly on one family name than the previous style of chart shown. Drafting this form of chart will take careful planning, using long and short vertical and horizontal lines to make best use of the space. Fig. 13 shows a family tree prepared in this form. It is the form of family tree most often used for families with very well documented histories, such as a branch of a royal family, but once you have decided at which point to stop your research on your own family name, it may be the style of chart you wish to have handwritten and framed.

Reading Fig. 13, what can you learn about the Smith family? The first known Smith was William Charles born in 1847 who married Sarah Ann Dean. They had three children: Samuel Charles, George William Joseph and William. (The name William appears throughout this family, with the two brothers George William and William presumably being named after their father. In the past, it was not unusual for parents to name a child after a deceased child who had died at a very early age. Sometimes the same name was given to several children of the same parents until one survived.)

George William Joseph, whose line we are following, married Emma Jane Sharpe and they had four children. Susan and Eliza have no birth or death dates. Checking with their

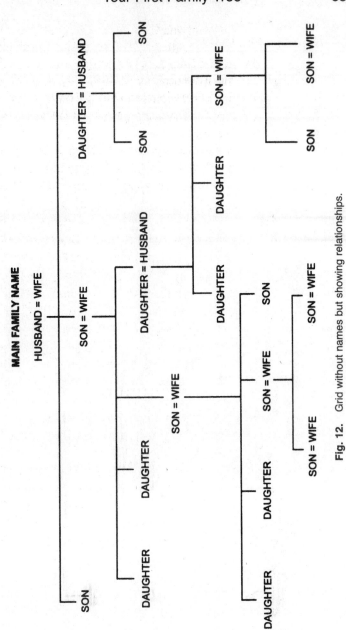

Fig. 12. Grid without names but showing relationships.

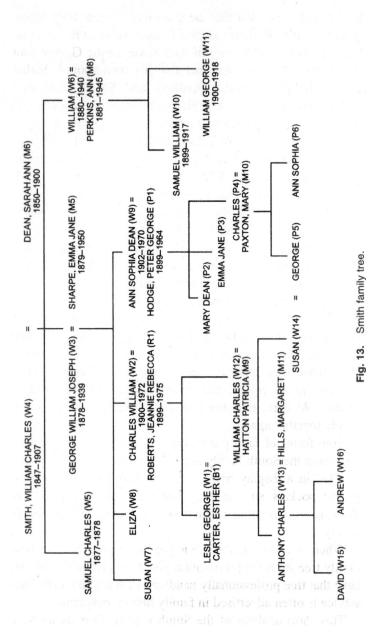

Fig. 13. Smith family tree.

index cards, we find that neither lived longer than a few weeks. Charles William married Jeannie Rebecca Roberts and they had two children one of whom was Leslie George (our researcher) who has also included his own spouse, Esther Carter, and his children, Anthony and Susan. Anthony's children are also shown, bringing us up to the present day and showing six generations of the Smith family.

The third child of William Charles and Sarah Ann was William who married Ann Perkins. Two children were born of that marriage, Samuel William and William George. Both Samuel William and William George died young leaving no issue, so that line of the Smith family died out. Looking at the dates of death of Samuel William and William George it would be reasonable to assume that they both died in the 1914–1918 war. This information would be shown on their index cards or in original or copy documentation.

Ann Sophia Dean Smith, daughter of George William Joseph and Emma Jane, sister of Charles William, married Peter Hodge and the family line of Hodge is followed. The reason for the inclusion of this new family name becomes clear when Ann Sophia Dean's grandson, George Hodge, marries Susan Smith, the granddaughter of her brother Charles William, thus bringing two branches of the Smith family together again.

Both forms of family tree, Figs. 11 and 13, give information about the Smith family and are complementary. They can be filed in a display book facing each other in two of the plastic pockets so that they can be read in conjunction showing a substantial amount of the history of the Smith family.

When you are satisfied that you have prepared the best family tree from the information you have gathered, you can have that tree professionally handwritten and illustrated. This service is often advertised in family history magazines.

This short analysis of the Smith Family Tree shows how

much we know about the family. When we have even more detailed information we can proceed to the writing of the history.

6

WHERE DO WE GO
FROM HERE?

Most beginners are able to find their own birth certificates and those of their parents, but what do you do if you are unable to get any further? If you cannot obtain the certificates you need to start you on your trail, what do you do?

Using your own birth certificate as a sample, go back to the beginning to look for clues and try to find your parents' marriage. If one of your parents had an uncommon surname, look for that name first since you will have less searching to do. If both have a fairly common name like Smith or Jones, concentrate on your father's name first. Usually your parents were married some time before your birth date – but not necessarily so. When you look into your family history, be prepared to learn many things you did not know – and for some shocks. You may unearth some family skeletons but your curiosity is natural and tracking a family history can reveal that some of our ancestors lived different or eccentric lives. How brave they were and worthy of admiration when they defied convention in a day and age when social behaviour which we now take for granted was considered outrageous and a scandal. You also have to take into account that registration may have taken place at a later date or in a different place.

Starting one year before your birth look for your father's name in the marriage indexes, systematically searching the indexes on the internet back from that date. When searching the indexes in this way, prepare your notes carefully so that you do not miss any pages. Write the names of the parties to the marriage at the top of a page in your notebook. Underneath the names write the first year you wish to check. Below that write each quarter for that year on a separate line. As you search, cross off each quarter in turn. There will be more than one image (page) for some quarters so make sure you check them all.

Although searching may take you some time at first, you will soon become quite practised and fairly quick. However, be thorough. Don't be tempted to skip through too quickly causing you to miss the vital names. In particular, make sure you always check the bottom of any page for any handwritten additions which may have been written there by the Registrar out of alphabetical order. Be aware that, since these *are* out of alphabetical order, the person who indexed the page for the internet may have misleadingly noted that name as the *last* name on the page. For example, when you search for a name in the indexes, the results page will offer you a list of pages, in each case stating which is the first name on that page and which is the last name on that page. If the last name on the page was actually Joe Smith but the name Jennifer Smith had been handwritten below Joe Smith on the page, the indexer may have simply noted Jennifer Smith as being the last name on the page. This would mislead you into thinking that there were no marriages at all for any Smith whose first name came between Jennifer and Joe.

The first time you try this form of searching you may feel frustrated and tempted to give up but the more you carry out these searches the easier it will become. When you find what you consider to be the correct entry, remember with marriages that you can cross check by looking for the marriage partner.

If the volume and page are the same you have found the correct entry. The indexes from 1912 onwards also give the name of the marriage partner which will give you an instant cross check.

If you are unable to find your father's name in your searches, look for your mother's name. In all cases make sure that you have the correct spelling and the correct first names. Many people are known in their family by names which are not the names under which they were registered. It can be quite surprising to learn that your mother who was always referred to as 'Cissie' by your father appears on her birth certificate as Alice Jane. If your father gave the information at the registration of your birth he may have given 'Cissie' as her name. If you have brothers or sisters and you know their dates of birth get a copy of their birth certificates and compare them with your own. They may show slight differences in spellings or names. Look to see who was the informant of the birth. If it was your mother on one of the certificates, her name is more likely to be correct on that one.

If a person had two first names such as Henry George but preferred the second, he may never have used his first name and always called himself George. He may have given the name by which he was known on his marriage certificate which could be different from that on his birth certificate. This did not invalidate the marriage. If they were married and the marriage registered, the marriage was valid even if they used a different name. Ages are often incorrect on marriage certificates, particularly if there was a marked difference in the age of the bride and groom or if the bride was under age and married without the consent of her parents.

If you are unable to find the marriage entry, consider other questions. Look outside the area. Were they married overseas or even at sea? If so search these indexes. The army records can also be a possible area for search. If no marriage can be found, be prepared for the fact that there never was a marriage to be registered and turn your search in another direction.

If you are looking for a birth entry consider the following question: are you looking in the right quarter or even the right year? Once again systematic searching, over a period of years either side of the year you think it is, might well be necessary. It is possible for several reasons that the baby was registered in the maiden name of the mother. If a first name had not been decided upon when registration took place the child would have been registered as 'male Smith' or 'female Smith' and would appear at the end of the entries for Smith. Don't forget the Miscellaneous indexes for babies born abroad. Many births in the early years of compulsory registration were not in fact registered so be prepared for that fact and search elsewhere.

There are also very often mistakes on death certificates since the informant may be a distant relative or a friend giving the information from hearsay. Check the information you have against all the other notes you have made concerning that person. If a widow remarries, the name on her death certificate will be her new surname. Once again don't forget the indexes for deaths abroad and deaths at sea.

Even with an uncommon surname it is possible to find more than one entry coupled with the same first name. If you find an entry with the name you are looking for, continue your search in case there is a similar name in the same period.

Other points to consider if you are unable to trace your missing relative are that the copy certificate you have received on which you are basing your search has been incorrectly copied from the original register. A name badly written in the original register could easily be misread by the person preparing the copy you have received. A name like 'Joan Crook' could easily be transcribed as 'Jane Cook'. The original registrar might have misheard what was said at the time of registration. All these things, some of them working together, can be very confusing for the family historian, but must be taken into account when a 'lost' relative cannot be found. If you are relying on addresses shown on the certificate as confirmation, 'Hart Street' could easily become 'Hurd Street'.

The original birth and death registers are held by local Registrars and it may be possible to search at those local registries, although most register offices do not have the facilities to allow the public to search their records. If you are not able to carry out a search yourself, the staff at the register office will carry out a search on your behalf for a statutory fee. Ring the register office or consult its website to find out the details and whether (if a search in person is allowed) you need to make an appointment and book a microfilm machine.

Some marriage registers, if the marriage took place in a church after 1837, are still held by the present incumbent of that church. Others may have been transferred to a local record office. An enquiry at the church should give the information as to where the original registers are now kept. Registers of civil marriages and of non Church of England marriages are held by the local Registrar.

If you discover that an error has been made on a copy certificate by the person copying the original register, you can return that copy to the General Register Office, pointing out the mistake and requesting a correct copy. However, if an incorrect entry is made in a register, whether it is a spelling error, an incorrect name or age, or even sex, it can currently only be corrected where it can be shown and established that an error was made at the time of registration. Correcting even the simplest spelling error requires formal procedures and the examination of appropriate evidence. However, the Government is proposing changes to the law to allow mistakes to be rectified more easily in future.

If you have any doubts about spellings, ages and names, ask in the family and check the notes you have made from the information you have gathered. It is possible to have several different spellings of a family surname over the generations, in which case other information is necessary to back up your view that the person included in your family history is entitled to be there.

Remember that everybody makes mistakes. Registrars, clerks and officials are no exception. They did and still do make mistakes. If you think you have found one, write to the local registrar or person responsible. Be polite but persistent, do not blame anyone, simply point out the error. If you cannot get a satisfactory answer, try further up the line of responsibility or ask for an interview to explain what you have found. You may be able to get the matter put right, or, if not, an acknowledgement in writing that a mistake has been made which you can use to support your own findings in your records.

If you are unable to proceed with your family history because you really cannot find a way through to the next generation, seek professional help. It is not always as expensive as you might think and a little help is always welcome. There are many professional genealogists and researchers, as in all professions, some good and some bad. Your local county record office will have a list of names and your local family history society may be able to help. Many advertise in genealogical magazines. In the UK there is an Association of Genealogists and Researchers in Archives (see Appendix) who have strict requirements for membership. Similarly, in the USA there is the Association of Professional Genealogists (again, see Appendix). In all cases ask for a list of their fees and charges. Most charge by the hour for work done plus expenses. If you decide to employ a professional agree a limit to the amount you wish to spend, requesting that when that limit is reached they do no more work without consulting you.

It is difficult to recommend a professional researcher since one person may find a researcher particularly helpful and another experience difficulties with the same person.

However, in the Appendix I do give the details of one researcher who I have found to be consistently careful and reliable. I take no responsibility if you choose to use his services but hope you will not be disappointed.

7

CENSUS RETURNS

A census of the population of England and Wales, Scotland, Northern Ireland, the Channel Islands and the Isle of Man has been taken every ten years (except in 1941 during the Second World War) since 1801. The first four censuses (1801, 1811, 1821 and 1831) simply consisted of a headcount of the population. Only in a very few instances did local enumerators list the actual householders' names. However, censuses from 1841 not only include the name and age of every person in the country, but also other additional information which makes the census returns one of the most important sources of information for the family history researcher. The census is compulsory, every house is visited and every person documented from babies one day old to the oldest in the land, giving a wealth of material for research.

The returns are released to the public after a hundred years. At present the years available to researchers are 1841, 1851, 1861, 1871, 1881, 1891 and 1901. The 1901 returns were made accessible on 1 January 2002 when for the first time they were also made available on the internet. The 1911 returns will be open in 2012.

When the 1881 returns became available, a long queue of anxious and excited researchers formed outside the Census Office overnight in order to be the first to obtain the information they were seeking. Whereas genealogists and family historians were once the only people interested in the census returns, historians and sociologists have now become aware of the value of the census and frequently use it as a basis for research into Victorian society and as a comparison to support their theories and researches relating to the present day. Fig. 14 shows a copy of a page from the 1881 census for Dartford.

The 1901 census was the first UK census to be made available on the internet in January 2002. Such was the demand for the information on the census website, it collapsed within hours of being launched. Now all the censuses from 1841 to 1901 can be accessed on the internet on sites such as Ancestry, 1901censusonline and FindMyPast. Generally, you can search these census websites by name free of charge and download and print actual images of the census entries for a small fee. Remember to save them on your computer so that you have a permanent copy.

At The National Archives in Kew you can access the 1901censusonline and Ancestry census material for the years 1841 to 1901 free of charge.

In addition, most local and county record offices have microfilm or microfiche copies of the census for their own areas. You can also arrange to look at the returns at the family history centres of the Church of Latter-day Saints (LDS). That organization has also made freely available on their Family Search website indexes of the 1881 British census, the 1880 USA and the 1881 Canadian censuses. The information was collected over a period of 11 years by an army of over 10,000 workers. For more information on how the Mormons can help you with your family history, see Chapter 11, page 133.

If your family was centred in one particular area, you may wish to purchase a CD which covers the area. Many county census records are now available for purchase from S & N Genealogy Supplies. Their complete list of products which include many other data CDs can be seen on their website.

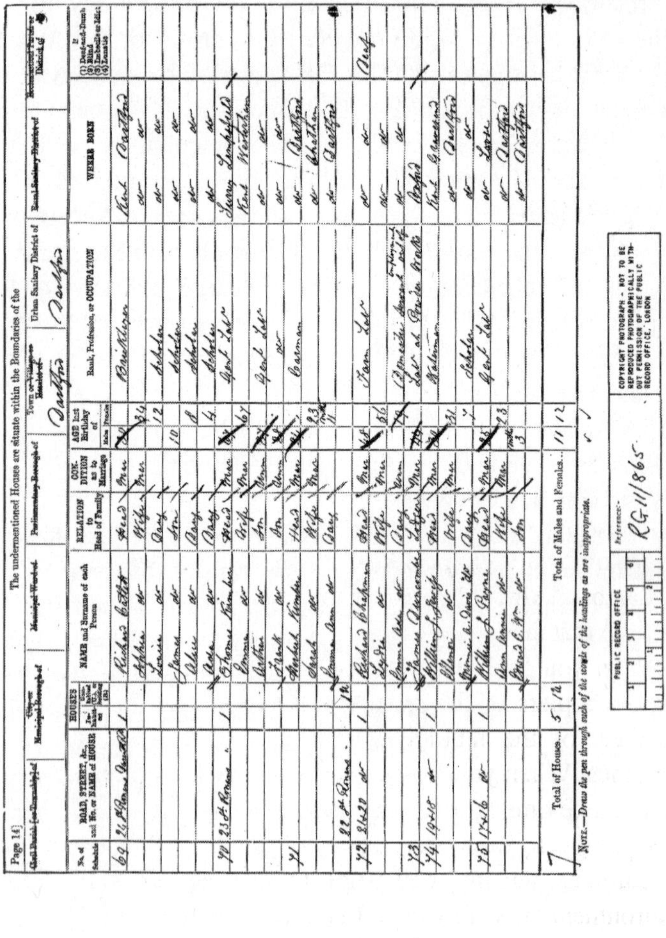

Fig. 14.   1881 census page. (The National Archives, ref. RG11/865, f.10, p.14).

It will help you to find your ancestors if you know where they were living on the day of the census, especially if they had a common name and a search on a census website brings up many possible candidates. Check the addresses you have been given by members of your family and found during your original research amongst family documents. In particular, check the addresses given on the birth, marriage and death certificates you have obtained. These will have a precise date; begin your research in the census year nearest to that date. The actual dates of the censuses were: 6 June 1841, 30 March 1851, 7 April 1861, 2 April 1871, 3 April 1881, 5 April 1891 and 31 March 1901.

If you cannot find your ancestors at the first attempt, do not despair. Search for alternative spellings of the name, bearing in mind that the name may have been spelt phonetically and not necessarily as spelt today. Many people in the nineteenth century had difficulty in reading and writing, and may have spelt their name differently at different times. Sometimes enumerators made transcription mistakes when they copied the names from the schedule completed by the householder into their notebook. Often the census returns are difficult to read which led to transcription errors by those who compiled the database which the census websites search to give a list of possible matches.

When you find an entry you are looking for, look at the other occupiers of the premises. Visitors or lodgers may be members of the family, in-laws or cousins with different surnames. When you look at the census returns for your own family, take time to look at the surrounding houses and build-ings, the occupations and names of neighbours, the sizes of the families. All this will begin to give you an idea of the environment in which they lived and the lives they led. In cities, many families herded together in single dwelling houses, others occupied large houses with servants. Work-house inmates are shown as well as hospital patients.

Occupations can also give an indication of the area in which people were living. Very often people engaged in the same or ancillary occupations grouped together and lived in one street. Street names were occasionally changed to reflect this. Fathers who had a trade taught their sons. Following through ten-year cycles, sons grow up, take over their fathers' occupations and themselves become 'Head of the house', although if a widowed mother is left she will sometimes be given as the 'Head of the house'. Apprentices lived with their masters, and many city dwellers let rooms to lodgers. In rural areas different branches of the same family lived near to each other and you could find a lead to take you on to another branch of the family. Sometimes you may be lucky enough to find visiting relatives or inlaws which can carry your research further.

The enumerators used abbreviations to save time and room on the forms when making their entries. Some of the more common abbreviations are:

Ag. Lab.	Agricultural labourer
Farm Lab.	Farm labourer
Gen. Lab.	General labourer
App.	Apprentice
Dom.	Domestic servant
H.	Head of household
Lab.	Labourer
N.K.	Not known
Serv.	Servant
dau.	daughter
inf.	infant
marr.	married
unmarr.	unmarried
wid.	widow
o.t.p.	of this parish

Most abbreviations are easily deciphered.

What Will You Find Out From the Census?

The 1841 census returns are the least informative, giving only the names of the occupants of each house, shop, hospital, workhouse and all occupied buildings on the night of 7 June 1841. Ages are not specific except for those under 15 years of age. Over 15 years, the ages are rounded up or down to the nearest five years. Divisions between families are shown and between houses and also occupations, but relationships, in which you are interested, are not shown. There is a column showing 'where born', in which initials are used. 'Y' means 'Yes, born in county of present residence', 'N' means 'No, not born in county of present residence', but no indication is given of where the person was actually born. 'I' means 'born in Ireland', 'S' means 'born in Scotland' and 'F' means 'born in foreign parts', again with no specific place of birth being given.

The returns for the following years are much more informative and are very helpful to the family historian. The details given in the years 1851 onwards are the names, the head of the house and the relationships to the head of the house of every other person present at the time of the census, whether they were married, their ages, occupations and exact places of birth. The 1851 and 1861 returns show those who were blind, deaf or dumb, and the 1871 and 1881 ones also indicate those who were idiots and lunatics.

Although people were supposed to answer the census questions truthfully, they did not always do so. The census entries were written by the enumerators and were either a copy of the form completed by the persons named or from the oral information given. Do not, therefore, rely entirely upon the information found in the census returns; check it against all the other information you have. Ages were often incorrect. If you are able to follow a female relative through several census returns, you may find that she remains the same age over a period of thirty years or mysteriously grows younger. I had one relative who in 1851 gave Scotland as his birthplace, in 1861 England and then in 1871 decided to give Scotland again. Such discrepancies can be confusing but, put together with all the other information you have gathered, will sort themselves out in the end and you should be able to decide which is the fact and which the fiction – but not always. There will always be question marks against some of the names in your family history.

When you look at the census, it will probably be the first time during your researches that you will see official records of different branches of your family in groups. Up until now, the certificates you have obtained have been either for one person or for two people if a marriage certificate.

Between one census and another, you may lose some people. Check the information given. They may have moved away or they may have died. If someone died, his or her spouse would be shown as widow or widower. This would give you a clue to the date of death if you do not already know it. It must have been between the dates of the two census returns. This would pinpoint the date more closely and possibly save much time searching the death records.

Look in the adjacent streets for their names. They may have been visiting a neighbour at the time the census was taken. The other alternatives are hospital, school or prison. Remember that house numbers, street names and boundaries may have changed between two censuses. If you have noticed the names of neighbours on previous censuses and they are still in occupation of adjacent houses, then your family must have moved away. If all the families have disappeared, they may be recorded elsewhere under a different street name.

Search each return from 1841 onwards, gradually assembling a picture of the family, its occupations and movements during those years.

Take a look at the marriage certificate of your grandparents or great-grandparents which you should have found without too much difficulty by following the instructions given in previous chapters. Once again using my Smith family as an example, we have the marriage of William Charles Smith and Sarah Ann Dean which took place in Dartford in Kent in 1876. The certificate gives the actual place of residence at the time of the marriage of both the bride and groom. The groom was living at 1 Mount Pleasant Road, Dartford, and the bride at Chalk Row, Dartford.

Taking the nearest census date, 2 April 1871, we can search for Sarah Ann Dean and William Charles Smith in Dartford. If they were living with their parents in their family homes at the time of the marriage, we will get more information about the family. If we search the previous 1861 census for them, we may learn even more about their relations, perhaps even discovering the names of their grandparents. Sometimes you may be lucky enough to find visiting relatives or in-laws which can carry your research further. Fig. 15 (on pages 84 and 85) is an example of what you might expect to see in the census returns.

The census returns for 1871 show that Sarah Ann Dean was living with her parents at Chalk Row, Dartford. Her father Alfred Dean was the head of the house, his age was 64, sex male, occupation army, and that he was born in Dartford. Her mother, Ann, is shown as 'wife'. Her age is 43, sex female, occupation housewife and place of birth Maidstone. All the children of the family are shown, including Sarah Ann – daughter, age 21, unmarried – whose occupation is shown as seamstress. An interesting point is that Sarah Ann and two of her brothers were born in India, probably while their father was in service in the army – a point well worth following. In addition to the family, there is an entry for Alice Brown, a servant, and William Cross, a lodger.

The birth certificate of George William Joseph, the son of Sarah Ann and William Charles, dated 1878, shows them living at 81 Mount Pleasant Road, East Hill, Dartford. A

PARISH OF HACKNEY

Name of Street, Place or Road and Name or No. of House	Name and Surname of each Person who abode in the house, on the Night of the 30th March 1851	Relation to Head of Family	Condition
21 Millfields Road	HENRY DANIEL	Head	Widower
	ELIZA DANIEL	Dau	Unm
	JOHN FOX	Lodger	Unm
	FRANK WILLIAM GREEN	Lodger	Unm
	ELEANOR CROSS	Serv	Mar
23 Millfields Road	SUSAN BERKLEY	Head	Mar
	HENRY HOLCOME	Son	Unm
	ALICE HOLCOMBE	Dau	Unm
	BENJAMIN BERKLEY	Son	Unm
	CHARLES BERKLEY	Son	Unm
25 Millfields Road	THOMAS SMITH	Head	Mar
	MARY SMITH	Wife	Mar
	JOAN BANKS	Niece	Unm

Fig. 15   What you might see in the 1851 Census return.

| Age of | | Rank, Profession or Occupation | Where born | Whether Blind or Deaf and Dumb |
male	female			
57		Manager at Bank	Norfolk, Norwich	
	27		Middlesex, London	
24		Bankers Clerk	Surrey, Old Kent Rd.	
40		Porter in a bank	Herts, Watford	
	30	Housekeeper	Kent, Dartford	
	38	Shop manageress	Middlesex, Hackney	
16		Scholar	Middlesex, Hackney	
	14	Scholar	Middlesex, Hackney	
12		Scholar	City of London	
8		Scholar	City of London	
39		Coalman	Middlesex, Tottenham	
	35		Northumberland, Newcastle	
	19		Northumberland, Newcastle	

search of the 1881 census for that house reveals all the family of Sarah Ann and William Charles, thus filling gaps in your family tree and spreading the branches further.

Scotland

The census returns for Scotland can be seen at New Register House in Edinburgh. A search charge is made and it is necessary to book in advance by letter, email or telephone in order to reserve a place. This does, however, eliminate a queue and the films are provided very quickly. Most of the census records are currently on microfilm but the returns for 1891 and 1901 have been digitized and can be viewed as images linked to indexes. The General Register Office for Scotland is in the process of digitising all its records to make them more easily available to the public both in their search rooms and also via the internet. At the time of writing, indexed census data is available from 1881 to 1901 on the ScotlandsPeople and Ancestry websites.

The original census returns for Scotland had to be sent to England and were then returned to Scotland. Unfortunately, parts of the 1841 census for the county of Fife were lost at sea on their way home and are not available in any form. If yours were lost, there is no alternative but to give up using the census for that line of research.

Ireland

Census records in Ireland can be seen at the National Archives in Dublin (see Appendix). These records have suffered losses caused, not only by fire, but also by deliberate destruction based on a decision made by the government, as in the case of the 1861 and 1871 records. There are, however, many census records still available to the family historian and you may well find what you are seeking. The 1911 census for Dublin is now online and other counties will follow, as will the 1901 census.

The Isle of Man

The census records of the Isle of Man are available at the Manx National Heritage Library (see Appendix) and can be purchased on CD. They can also be accessed on the Ancestry website. A useful piece of information given on these records is the place of birth of the person recorded. If the person was born off the island, the country of birth is given.

The Channel Islands

The census records for the Channel Islands are available online on the Ancestry website. The census records for Jersey are also available at the library of the Société Jersiaise, the Jersey Archive and the Jersey Public Library (see Appendix). Those for Guernsey, Alderney and Sark may be searched on microfilm at the Greffe in St Peter Port.

The 1911 Census

Limited access to the 1911 census is now available. For a fixed fee, it is possible to research addresses on this census. Application can be made via a link on The National Archives website or by post to The National Archives. In addition to information available on previous censuses, the 1911 census indicates nationality, and how long people have been married.

8

PARISH REGISTERS

When you have exhausted all the research sources offered by civil registration records, where can you look for pre-1837 information? There are many pre-registration sources. The details gained from your census research and copy certificates can lead you to probably the most important which are the parish registers.

Parish registers, which were handwritten, contain records of baptisms, marriages and burials and were instituted in 1538 by Thomas Cromwell, during the reign of Henry VIII. They relate to the established Church of England. However, all the earliest registers have not been preserved, and you may find that the records of the parish in which you are interested start much later. The information given in each register was at the discretion of the parish clerk and may vary from parish to parish and from year to year in each parish. A diligent and conscientious clerk would give the maximum and a lazy clerk the minimum.

The parish registers were normally in the charge of the vicar or incumbent of each church, but in 1979 a law was enacted to ensure the protection and preservation of parochial records. If a local incumbent was not able to keep the documents in a suitably safe environment the records had to be deposited elsewhere in a record office covering the diocese of that church. The usual place was the county record office.

The diocesan record offices also have the power to request that any parish registers still held by a local incumbent be deposited with them on loan for a period of one year.

Under the 1979 law, county record offices may not make an inspection charge for parish registers deposited with them, although they may have a general search fee and a fee for use of microfilm and microfiche machines. Incumbents are allowed to charge a fixed inspection fee. Incumbents are legally bound to allow any registers they hold to be inspected, but they have no duty to search the registers themselves in response to requests by letter. However, many will do so but although they may be willing, they may not be experienced or efficient researchers. They may miss just the point that you are seeking to confirm. If you seek their assistance a donation to the church funds sent with the request would probably be appreciated.

If you wish to inspect a parish register, ask the local record office whether they hold that register. If they do not, they will be able to advise the name and address of the incumbent who does hold that register, or any other place where it is held. If you require the name and address of the present incumbent of any parish church, this can be obtained from *Crockford's Clerical Directory*, which should be available in your local reference library, or by searching online.

If the register is still held by the incumbent, write (enclosing a stamped addressed envelope for reply) or telephone or email in advance of your visit, requesting an appointment and listing the registers you wish to inspect. This will help the incumbent and also save time, which may be limited.

Make a list for yourself, chronologically, which is the way the registers are kept, and by name. Include the surnames of all the families you are researching, cousins, in-laws and any other relatives so that you can make the most use of your visit. Do not forget the ever important notebook and pencils, magnifying glass and money to pay for copies and fees.

Make a very careful and exact copy of the records you find,

together with a note of the source and references in case you wish to return for further research. Follow exactly the names, spellings, and dates even if they are different from what you expected to find. You could also use a digital camera to record the data if that is allowed. In most record offices you can obtain photocopies of the pages of the parish registers, which can be added to your supporting documents file.

Note all the references to your surname however remote the relationship might seem; they may well fit into your family tree somewhere on a distant branch.

It is essential to search all the registers of a parish, commencing with the latest and working back to the earliest. Do not assume that you have a complete record from one parish register. Families moved about then as they do now. They could have left the parish before all the children were born, or come to the parish from another bringing some children baptised elsewhere with them.

Parish registers can, like the census returns, reveal the way of life followed by our ancestors. How large families were, how they moved about, how long people lived. A sudden increase in burials one year could indicate an illness sweeping through a parish or a bad winter. There is much more to be learned from parish registers than names, dates and places.

Parish Register Copies
Many parish registers have been copied, with some copies available in printed form. The printed copies can be seen in county record offices, libraries and the Society of Genealogists in London. Local family history societies sometimes hold copies relating to the parishes in their own areas. These should only be used as an aid since as with all transcriptions they do contain errors and omissions but they are helpful as a guide to where to look and what records exist.

Searching the internet for information on the parish register you are interested in and searching a specialist genealogical site such as GENUKI should provide details of what is available and where.

You may be lucky and find that the parish register you want to see has been digitized and is available on CD or online. S & N Genealogy Supplies have transcribed some parish records and produced searchable databases which are available for a fee on The Genealogist website. Where they have permission they try to reproduce an image of the original page.

Bishops' Transcripts
Commencing with the year 1597, a full copy of each parish register had to be sent to the diocesan bishop each year. Many of the Bishops' Transcripts, referred to by family historians and genealogists as 'BTs', are easier to read than the original parish registers and are available at county record offices sometimes on microfilm or microfiche. There are also some BTs commencing in 1561 but these are not comprehensive. All the BTs for Wales are held in the National Library of Wales (see Appendix).

Bishops' Transcripts are by no means complete records since parish clerks did not always comply with the instructions given. In addition mistakes were made by the parish clerks in transcriptions from the registers, and full returns were not always made. They may be helpful however, if original parish registers have been lost. Many Bishops' Transcripts were lost or destroyed, including those for the diocese of St Paul's Cathedral, lost in the Great Fire of London in 1666. BTs should be used as an aid, and any entries found should be checked with the original parish registers if possible.

The Calendar

It is important to know that before 1751, following the Julian calendar, the church year began on Lady Day 25 March and ended the following 24 March. The Gregorian calendar then came into use giving 1 January as the first day of the year and 31 December the last. In order to catch up with the alterations in the calendar, in 1751 25 March became the first day of the year and 31 December the last, giving 1751 only 9 months. In 1752 the year commenced on 1 January and ended on 31 December, but 14 September followed 2 September leaving out 11 days. In 1753 and from then onwards the year began on 1 January and ended on 31 December. When recording entries between 1 January and 24 March for the years prior to 1750, both the old and present day style of dating should be shown. For example, 23 February 1731 should be shown as 23 February 1731/1732, the historical date being 1732 but the church date being 1731. (This applies *only* to the dates between 1 January and 24 March.)

Kings and Queens

Some early documents do not give an exact date, but refer to a time in the life of the reigning monarch. For example, 'on the twelfth day of August in the ninth year of the reign of our Gracious Queen Elizabeth'. This requires a little extra research into the exact date the monarch in question ascended to the throne. The reign of George IV commenced on 29 January 1820, making the year 29 January 1820 to 28 January 1821 the first year of his reign, and 29 January 1822 to 28 January 1823 the third year of his reign. The practice of dating documents using what are known as regnal years was not used during the Interregnum or Commonwealth years (1649 to 1660) and ceased after the reign of Queen Victoria whose first year as Queen began on 20 June 1837. After the restoration of the monarchy, at the end of the Interregnum, the reign of

Charles II was backdated to the death of Charles I and was deemed to have commenced on 30 January 1649. You can find tables giving the exact dates of regnal years by searching on the internet and looking in appropriate reference books in your local library.

The Marriage Act 1753
In 1754 an Act promulgated in 1753 by the then Lord Chancellor, Lord Hardwicke, was enforced. The Act, which covered England and Wales, was designed to reduce the number of clandestine marriages. It standardized the performance of marriages and the entries to be made in parish registers. Parents or guardians had to give consent to marriages of minors. Banns had to be called or marriage licences issued before a marriage could take place in a church or chapel, failing which the marriage had to be entered in the register on printed forms, thus providing more information for the family historian. The Act did not affect those of the Jewish or Quaker faiths who were allowed to marry within their own religions provided a proper register was kept. Roman Catholics were not excluded from the Act. This Act led to clandestine but legal marriages taking place over the border in Scotland where the consent of parents to a minor's marriage was not required. If you are unable to find a marriage record you are seeking in a local parish register, don't forget Gretna Green in Scotland where many marriages took place. A couple might then return to their parish where no record of their marriage existed, but the birth of their first child might show in the parish register, leaving the family historian with a missing piece of the puzzle. Until 1929 boys were allowed to marry with parental consent from the age of 14 years and girls with consent from the age of 12, so do not be surprised at the dates of marriages compared with birth dates. In 1929 the minimum age for marriage for both boys and girls became 16 years. These

points should be taken into consideration when searching for marriages.

During the period of the Civil War and the Commonwealth that followed, between 1642 and 1660, bishops were abolished and the keeping of registers was abandoned by many parishes. Licences were not issued and marriages were performed under civil law by authorized ministers, JPs and magistrates. There is therefore a fairly large hole in the run of parish registers.

Baptisms

The information in parish registers relates to baptisms – not births. If a child was not baptised there will be no record of the birth in the parish register. There are a number of reasons why a baptism did not take place. The parents could have been non-conformists, Quakers, Jews or Roman Catholics. A baptism could have taken place in a nearby parish if, as was common, a young wife returned to her mother's house for help with the birth of her child. A child born in a city to country-born parents may have been taken back to the country parish for baptism. Not all baptisms took place near the time of the birth. Sometimes if a child was born early in a marriage the parents could not afford the baptism fee. As they prospered and the family grew, all the children could be baptised at the same time some years after the birth of several of them, in which case their respective ages may be given. Some baptisms refer to adults and not children. If you are doubtful, try to check elsewhere. The BTs might help. Illegitimate children were often baptised and reference made in the register to their illegitimacy with, occasionally, the father also named.

The information given for a baptism will be the date, Christian names of the child, parents' Christian names with the father's surname (mother's surname for an illegitimate child), by whom baptised and may sometimes also include the mother's maiden name, where they lived (village or town) and profession of father.

It was not compulsory to give the age at baptism and often that information was omitted, making it difficult for the family historian to find an exact date of birth from parish registers. It was the baptism which was important at that time, not the age of the person being baptised. It may be necessary to try to find evidence of exact dates elsewhere if possible, from monumental inscriptions, family Bibles, other family documentation or entries in the parish registers relating to other members of the family. Dates and ages were not so important in parish registers which were meant to be records of religious events.

Marriages

Marriages are more likely to be shown in parish registers than are baptisms, since most were performed by the Church, although not always in the expected parish. From 25 March 1754 onwards the banns had to be called or licences issued. Banns had to be called in the parish of the proposed bride and groom and the marriage could have taken place in either parish. It was only necessary to have been a resident in a parish for three weeks to enable a marriage to take place. One or other of the couple might come from a distant parish or a travelling couple could have decided to remain in a parish for the purpose of marriage and then moved on again. If you are unable to find the entry in the groom's parish, look for it in the bride's parish where the marriage was more likely to have taken place. Banns were usually entered in a separate banns book, but could be entered in the marriage register separately from the marriages. If a marriage was by licence (which gave permission to marry without the calling of the banns) the fact would be recorded in the register. An application for a licence would have been for a licence bond or allegation and either made to a bishop or an archbishop's office. If a register entry shows a marriage by licence, search for the bond or allegation which will give further genealogical information. If there is one, obtain a photocopy for your documents file. Marriages by licence became quite the fashion in all walks of life, although the licences themselves no longer exist since they were given to the bride and groom when issued and have been lost through the ages.

A marriage entry in a parish register from 25 March 1754 should give the names of both parties, the occupation of the groom, the names of their respective parishes, and their status (spinster, widow, bachelor, widower). If the bride is shown as a widow, remember that her surname will be that of her former husband and not the family surname, leaving you with further research. If either or both of the parties to the marriage were minors and the marriage was by consent of parents or guardians, that fact will be shown. This would show that the consenting parent was alive at the time of the marriage, another piece of useful information. The names of two and sometimes three witnesses are also given in the register. These are of particular interest as they could be other members of the family. If the same name as a witness appears at other marriages in the register this may have been a professional witness or the parish clerk. It is worth checking the surrounding marriages if only to eliminate that name from your researches.

The Society of Genealogists holds 'Boyd's Marriage Index' which, in a series of volumes, indexes marriages in several counties from 1538 to 1837. Copies of this index on microfilm can be seen in some county record offices and reference libraries, and is available online to subscribers to the British Origins website.

Burials

The information in parish registers relates to burials – not deaths, although burials usually took place within a few days of the death. Once again the deaths of nonconformists, Quakers, Jews and Roman Catholics will probably not be entered. The information given in relation to a burial is often only the name and age of the deceased and the date of burial. Other information shown might in the case of a female be 'widow or wife of . . .' and in the case of children 'son or daughter of . . .'

A useful index to burials in England and Wales is the National Burial Index. This is a project originated in 1994 by the Federation of Family History Societies whereby members of various family history societies and some other individuals are transcribing the burial registers for their area. The index is available on CD, with a new updated edition produced at roughly three-year intervals. Many of the entries in the index, along with some others, can be searched on the FindMyPast website.

Other Registers

If your ancestors were followers of a religion other than that of the established Church of England, they were known as non-conformists or dissenters and were excluded from many laws, such as Hardwicke's Marriage Act of 1753.

Roman Catholics

Registers of births and marriages, often written in Latin, were kept by Roman Catholic churches and some still remain in the possession of the priest in charge of local churches. Some registers are held in The National Archives or have been deposited in local county record offices. Roman Catholics were frequently buried in local parish churchyards and their burials were recorded in the general parish registers. If you wish to trace an ancestor of the Roman Catholic religion, contact the archivist of the Roman Catholic diocese concerned. He will know the present whereabouts of the parish registers. Alternatively, the Catholic Family History Society (see Appendix) may be able to help you with your research. Also the Catholic National Library (see Appendix) currently holds Mission Registers (listing baptisms, confirmations, marriages and deaths) dating back to 1694.

Jews
Jews lived in many parts of England, but the largest community was in London. Most synagogues kept records of their congregations. Some Jews paid for their children to be included in local parish registers. If such entries were made they stated 'son or daughter of a Jew'. There are many such entries in parish registers of City of London churches. Marriages were not always recorded, but brides had to be given a marriage contract and often deposited copies with the synagogue. Burials were recorded in the records of Jewish burial grounds. For information of the records available, write to the synagogue in the area in which you are interested, asking what documentation is available. There is also a Jewish Museum in London (see Appendix) where original records can be seen.

Quakers – The Society of Friends
The Quakers kept extensive and informative records. Some of their records have been deposited at county record offices and some of the original births, marriages and burials are held at The National Archives. Microfilms of those digested copies can be seen at the Library of the Society of Friends in London (see Appendix) upon payment of a small fee.

Protestant Non-Conformists

Baptists, Methodists, Presbyterians, United Reformed Churches and Congregationalists, all kept records of the births, marriages and deaths of their congregations. Here again some records have been deposited with local county record offices and some with The National Archives. Many remain with the local congregations. Write to the local chapel or church asking for information as to the whereabouts of the documents you are seeking. There is a Baptist Historical Society and a Methodist Archive Collection (in Manchester). (See Appendix.)

Huguenots

Huguenots were French, but many also came to England from Holland or Germany. They settled mainly in London, Bristol, Canterbury, Colchester, Norwich, Plymouth, Rye, Sandwich and Southampton. Their records have been deposited in local county record offices and The National Archives. If there was no local French church, baptisms were carried out by the local parish church and the records appear in parish registers. Deaths generally are not documented except for those that occurred at the London Huguenot Hospital. Check with the local archives to see what is available or contact the Huguenot Library in London (see Appendix).

Scotland

The parish registers in Scotland can be seen on microfilm at New Register House in Edinburgh. A search fee is charged and it is necessary to make an appointment as in the case of searching the civil registration records. However, since all the records are under one roof, one day may cover a great deal of research. At the time of writing, computerized indexes to the births/baptisms and proclamations/marriages are currently available on the ScotlandsPeople website, with those for deaths/burials expected to be made available in the near future.

Not many parish registers survive before 1700. There are more registers for Glasgow and Edinburgh than for country areas. The information given for baptisms often includes the maiden name of the mother which is helpful. Some registers have been indexed and transcribed. The Society of Genealogists in London holds copies of some areas of Scotland on microfilm.

Ireland

Many parish registers in Ireland were deposited in the Irish Record Office in Dublin and were destroyed by fire in 1922. Do not be put off by this generalization concerning Irish records. Many records were transcribed and copied locally before they were sent to Dublin and some were not sent to Dublin at all. Copies of most of the parish registers are available in Dublin at the National Library (see Appendix). There are registers for both Catholic and Protestant churches. The Catholic registers are usually written in Latin and some help may be required in translation.

Original registers are usually held by local parish priests and parish clerks and the usual written approach can be made. Try the local parish priest by writing, setting out clearly the information you are seeking. You cannot expect a busy parish priest to do your research for you, or he may not have the expertise, but a polite request accompanied by a contribution to the upkeep of the church may bring a very helpful response. There are many parish registers on microfilm and some local family history societies have detailed information concerning their parish registers.

While on the subject of Ireland, if you have any form of enquiry and you know the parish concerned, it is always a good idea to write to the present parish priest. He is usually very knowledgeable about his own area and its history or can point you in the right direction. A written request accompanied by a reply paid envelope and a donation to church funds often produces a great deal of information concerning the history of a family.

Useful websites for those researching Irish ancestors include the Irish Ancestors website of the *Irish Times* and the From Ireland website.

On the Public Record Office of Northern Ireland website (see Appendix) there are indexes of the Church of Ireland and Presbyterian Church registers held on microfilm.

Isle of Man

Copies of parish registers on microfilm or microfiche can be seen at the Manx National Heritage Library. Many original parish registers can be seen at the Civil Registry. An enquiry made to the Civil Registry or the Library will enable you to find out where the original registers are held and what is available. The usual stamped addressed envelope is not of much help since the Isle of Man has its own postage stamps. A postal order to cover the cost of postage or an international reply paid coupon can be used.

The Channel Islands

Parish registers in the Channel Islands are mostly still held by the incumbents of the local churches in Jersey, Guernsey and the other islands. Write first to the present incumbent to ask which records he now holds or whether he knows where the records you are seeking are held. The usual stamped addressed envelope is not of much help since the Channel Islands have their own postage stamps. An international reply paid coupon available from your own post office should be used.

If you are directed by your searches to other religions, always write to the local church, chapel or meeting house (with the usual stamped addressed envelope for reply) stating that you are compiling a family history and what records you are seeking. If they do not hold the records themselves they will almost certainly know where they have been deposited or be able to direct you where else to apply.

9

WILLS, PROBATE AND
MONUMENTAL INSCRIPTIONS

Wills provide a very important source of information for the
family historian since they often contain references to several
members of the family, even when they are excluded, giving
their full names and relationships to the deceased person,
known as the testator (male) or testatrix (female). The name
and address of the person asked to administer the will,
executor (male) or executrix (female), would also be
included. If a beneficiary was a distant relative or one who
had moved away, the address might also be given. A will
could also introduce you to a previously unknown member
of the family or show a connection with a distant branch. If
there was no will, but property (the estate) was left, a
member of the family or several of them together could apply
to be executors by means of letters of administration which
took the place of a will. In this case the full names and
addresses of the proposed executors together with their relationship to the deceased would be given. A will could also
give guidance as to the place of burial where a tombstone
or monument might give the names of other members of the
family and family relationships.

Many people, even the poorest, made wills, some of them

being 'deathbed wills' dictated to a close friend or church representative just prior to death. Women bequeathed their 'best bonnet with the blue ribbons', 'my large copper pan' or 'my second best grey woollen skirt'. Men bequeathed 'my milking cow with calf', 'one shilling' or 'my heavy working coat'. Blankets and feather beds were frequently bequeathed as were single items of furniture such as chairs, dressers and beds. It may seem an odd thing to say, but wills can bring your ancestors to life in many ways. The value of the goods bequeathed can indicate how highly the testator thought of the recipient. Lists or inventories of possessions indicate the wealth of the family and sometimes its standing in the community. I recently assisted a local archive to sort and catalogue a bundle of early handwritten wills, most of which had not been inspected before. The time spent on this work was most rewarding, bringing to light the environment in which people were living. One will was made by a widow who had been a shopkeeper and the inventory attached gave the total contents of the shop, which was a general store, together with all the prices. As I read the will, I could see her in my mind's eye weighing bags of flour and oats, measuring off yards of blue sprigged muslin and lavender silk and dispensing molasses and rum. Another will gave minute details of all the dresses bequeathed by an obvious lady of fashion to her daughters and friends.

Family quarrels can be referred to. Members of the family can be included or excluded by name giving their relationship to the testator. Next of kin could contest a will if they had been excluded, thereby delaying the execution of the bequests. It became the custom to leave a small amount, usually six pence to a disliked relative so that he could not object, giving rise to the saying 'cut off with a sixpence'.

Before 1882, when a woman married, her possessions and property became the possessions and property of her husband and at her death she had no right to bequeath any of her belongings. Therefore before that date not many women made wills, unless they were widows. In 1882 a law was passed giving married women rights over their own possessions and from that date you may find wills by both male and female members of your family.

Fig. 16 (overleaf) is a copy of a will of William Catlett of Sittingborne, one of my husband's ancestors, proved in the Prerogative Court of Canterbury in 1647. It was written by him in 1646 and a death bed codicil was added in 1647. William obviously tried to remember everyone he could think of and mentions no less than thirty-four people by name as well as the poor of five different parishes. This will gives many relationships and some parishes where people lived. It is also of assistance in tracing family members since it clearly identifies married women by their maiden and married surnames. The occupations of some beneficiaries are also given. As you will see, this will provides many hours of research if all the names and relationships are to be followed and checked in parish registers. Even those mentioned without giving the relationships have to be checked in case they are family members or for the purposes of elimination if they are not.

It is, of course, necessary to know the date or approximate date and place of death in order to start looking for a will. For pre-registration dates, parish registers may give this information. From the date of compulsory registration, with diligent searching the date of death can be found in the death indexes. Census records can also give a clue. If an elderly person in the family 'disappears' in the ten years between one census return and the next while all the other members of the family can be found, a reasonable assumption is that he or she has died. This is not always the case, but you could narrow your first search to that period of ten years. Newspaper announcements can also give information relating to deaths and burials. Personal columns sometimes carry entries of anniversaries of deaths

Copy Will of William Catlett, 1646

William Catlett of Sittingborne co. Kent gentleman dated 15 March 1646.

To poor of Sittingborne £5.00, of Milton £5.00, of Fong 40/–, of Bapchild 40/–, of Podmersham 40/–.

To Edward Gurland of Sittingborne clerk £5.00. To Mr. Lane of Bridgar clerk £5.00. To Mr. Picard clerk of Bapchild 40/–. To my niece Dickerson of Faversham widow £20.00. To my niece Sampson £20.00. To my cousin John Bix of Bapchild Esq £10.00 and to William his son and to Katherine his daughter £10.00 a piece. To my cousin Nicholas Ady £20. To my cousin Elizabeth Adye alias Smith, sister to said Nicholas £40.00. To my cousin George Hicks £10.00. To my cousin Adye Hicks £10.00. To my cousin Elizabeth Frinde £10.00. To my cousin Ann Bradley alias Brockwell £20.00. To my cousin Elizabeth Bradley alias Upton £10.00. To my cousin William Bradley £20.00. To my cousin William Allen of Morston £10.00. To my cousin Allen of Sittingborne, tailor, £5.00. To my cousin Edward Tomlyn of

Fig. 16   Copy will of William Catlett.

Sittingborne £10.00 To my cousin Thomas Currall of Rochester, boatswain £20.00. To Robert Currall and Thomas Currall sons of said Thomas £10 a piece. To Elizabeth Currall daughter of said Thomas Currall £20.00. To John Pawson of Sittingborne £30.00. To my servant Elizabeth Midler £20.00. To Henry Lawrence £10.00. To Solomon Bowell £10.00. To my cousin William Catlett of Fong £20. To my cousin Richard Catlett, son of said William £20.00. To my cousin Susan Allen alias Lambert £10.00. To John Lambert of Blackwale, husband of said Susan 40/-. To my cousin George Catlett of Blackwale £20.00. To John Clench of Starfield £5.00. To Jane Burges alias Sharpe £5.00.

Nuncipat Codicil made about 12 o'clock at night after Tuesday 19 October 1647.

Being put to mind by Samuel Packer on that very night attended on him of some about him that had done him service and that he did not or had not remembered them they would condemn him. Testator said he had done so and given something to poor but not much. Asked who should be executor he answered his cousin John Bix of Bapchild Esq.

Witness. Samuel Packer and John Pawson both of Sittingborne.

Probatum 23 October 1647 by said witnesses and John Bix executor.

paid for by a surviving spouse or son or daughter whose names and relationships are also given.

Pre-Registration Wills Before 1858

Many wills were never proved or lodged for registration anywhere, either because it was not necessary to do so, or the estate was not large enough to warrant the expense. Even when registration became compulsory there was (and still is) no requirement to prove or register a will or letters of administration with a value below a certain amount. Where there were family disputes, there might be several years' delay between the date of death and the proving of a will or letters of administration.

Original early wills can be found in many places. Before January 1858 when wills and letters of administration came under the jurisdiction of the Principal Probate Registry, wills could be proved in ecclesiastical or church courts, the main courts being the Prerogative Court of Canterbury (PCC) and the Prerogative Court of York (PCY).

Records of wills for the PCY are held at the Borthwick Institute of York (see Appendix, page 177). However, published indexes to these wills for the years 1389–1688 are available at The National Archives at Kew.

Records of wills for the PCC are held at The National Archives. Microfilm copies of PCC wills and administrations for the years 1384–1858 can be searched at Kew. There are printed indexes of wills up to 1800, and 1853–1858; and there are printed indexes of administration grants 1559–1660, 1701–1749 and 1853–1858. Wills and administrations for other dates can be found through annual initial indexes. Images of the wills proved by the PCC in the years 1384 to 1858 can be downloaded from The National Archives website for a fee.

The British Origins website provides access on subscription to some will indexes, including an index to PCC wills for

1750–1800 and an index to the wills of the Archdeaconry Court of London 1700–1807.

It is possible, where a testator left property in more than one parish, that his will came under the jurisdictions of both the PCC and the PCY. Searching for early wills is difficult even if they were proved, since it is necessary to decide in which court the will might have been proved. Start by a process of elimination, searching all the indexes of all the courts known to cover a particular parish where the testator died.

If no wills appear in either the PCC or PCY records, they could appear in the records of the lower courts, many of which are held in local county record offices. Bundles of wills deposited by churches and solicitors are also held by county record offices and local archives. The Society of Genealogists also holds many documents deposited with it by private persons. Other sources of pre-registration wills are detailed in the leaflet relating to wills and probate available from The National Archives. Pre-registration wills for Wales are held in the National Library of Wales, while those for Scotland and those for Ireland are held in each country's National Archives.

Wills from 1858

Wills from January 1858 onwards are much easier to find. All wills and letters of administration proved in England and Wales are held at the Principal Registry of the Family Division (Probate Registry) in London (see Appendix).

The wills are indexed chronologically with surnames in alphabetical order for each year. Base your search of the index on the date of death obtained from the death certificate, remembering that it could be some years after the date of death that a will or letters of administration are proved. The indexes also give such information as the value of the estate, the address of the testator and the names of the executors. There is no fee charged for a search of the indexes. You can inspect copy wills after paying a fee and submitting an application form – there is a notice in the index room telling you how to apply. You will be able to take notes from the wills (using pencil), and remember to make a careful record of the source of your information, with any references, in case you wish to return for further research. A photocopying service is also available on payment of a fee per page copied, either to be collected personally or mailed to you. You may like to have copies of the original wills, showing your ancestors' signatures, and these can also be ordered, for a fee. Your order form should clearly state that a copy of the original will is required.

Indexes to wills and administrations from 1858–1943 are available on microfiche at The National Archives at Kew.

If you aren't able to get to First Avenue House, you can order copies of wills and administrations by post from the York Probate Sub-Registry. See Appendix.

Scotland

From 1824 onwards, wills for Scotland were proved in the local sheriff's court where they may still be held. Otherwise they are all deposited at The National Archives of Scotland (see Appendix). Scottish wills from 1513–1901 have been digitized by the Scottish Archive Network (SCAN). An index to these wills is available on the ScotlandsPeople website where the wills can be downloaded for a fee.

Ireland

Irish wills are once again difficult to trace since many were destroyed in 1922. Indexes, even of those destroyed, do exist and are held in the National Archives in Dublin. An index to Irish wills, for the years 1484–1858, is available on CD-Rom at The National Archives at Kew. The Irish Origins website has an index of over 102,000 Irish wills from 1484 to 1858.

Isle of Man

All the early wills from 1631 are held on microfilm in the Manx National Heritage Library. There are also original wills held in the archives which have not yet been indexed. Wills commencing in 1916 are held in the General Registry Office and the originals can be inspected. There is a search fee payable at the Registry.

The Channel Islands

Wills and probate records for the Channel Islands are held at the Jersey Archive in St Helier for Jersey and at the Greffe in St Peter Port for Guernsey and the other Channel Islands.

When searching any indexes for wills it is sensible to take time to search each year for all wills under the family surname which you are currently researching. You may come across a will which looks as though it belongs to you, the address of the deceased or the names of the executors pointing to an association with a known member of your family. You need only request a sight of the originals of those that seem markedly of interest.

When you have found your will or letters of administration, extract as much information as you can to enter in your notebook and transfer to your index cards. Make a note of where the will is kept, the date you saw it and reference number ascribed to the document in case you should need to refer to it again at a later date. Important facts to look for are the following:

1. Name of testator/testatrix.
2. Occupation of the testator.
3. Date of will, date of death and date of grant of probate, which could all be different.
4. Address of the testator when the will was made.

5. Names and addresses of executors and relationship to the testator if given.
6. Names and addresses of all beneficiaries with relationships to testator and to each other (wife, children, brothers, sisters, etc.).
7. Names of people excluded by definition and relationship to testator.
8. Names, addresses and occupations of the witnesses to the signature of the testator. Witnesses are not allowed to be beneficiaries under a will and possibly will be neighbours, solicitors or their clerks or members of the clergy, not necessarily related to the family. A full note should be taken, if only for the purposes of elimination.
9. Any burial instructions given.
10. Any special bequests, particularly land or houses, that might prove a point of interest for your family history write-up.

If you find some pages of particular interest, such as those with the signatures, names and relationships of beneficiaries or unusual bequests, ask for a photocopy for your documents books.

Cemeteries and Monumental Inscriptions
Your researches amongst parish registers, wills and newspapers (see page 129) should enable you to find the burial places of some of your ancestors. Death certificates may also give you a clue. Give yourself the pleasure on a bright summer's day of a visit to a churchyard or cemetery. If the parish registers you are seeking are still held by the local church you could combine the register research with a visit to the churchyard.

Unfortunately inscriptions on old tombstones, which can suffer from pollution, vandalism, weathering and general neglect, are fast becoming unreadable. Churchyards are also being cleared and 'tidied up'. If you find evidence of a burial, make a visit to the churchyard or cemetery a priority amongst your researches before destruction takes place. Take a camera with you. You may be able to obtain pictures of gravestones with monumental inscriptions (usually referred to by family historians and genealogists as MIs) for your documents books before they are gone for ever. Many local family history societies are recording MIs and have recorded some that have now disappeared. Contact the appropriate local society to enquire whether they have any records relating to the church-yard in which you are interested. It should be borne in mind that not all burials had tombstones and tombstones were sometimes erected in memory of people who died abroad, particularly members of the forces killed in action. MIs can also appear on public war memorials, inside churches on pews which have been dedicated by a family and in stained glass church windows. Local war memorials in particular should not be overlooked since they could give a clue to a missing person whose death you have been unable to establish.

Due to the rapid increase in population, churchyards became overcrowded particularly in cities. By 1820 the overcrowding of churchyards in London reached epidemic proportions and private graveyards or cemeteries began to appear. They were not subject to the same controls as church-yards and their upkeep was generally in the hands of private individuals. Many have since disappeared or been incorporated into public gardens. Local authorities were empowered to establish cemeteries and other cemeteries, such as the famous Highgate Cemetery in London, were set up by companies who sold burial plots on a profit-making basis. Some churchyards, local authority cemeteries and the private company cemeteries kept plans, numbering each grave and entering the names of the persons buried. Highgate Cemetery which closed in 1975 has records from 1839 showing how burial plots passed from one member of a family to another, the size of the plots and the cost, including descriptions of the memorial stones erected. These records are very helpful if they can be found. Often they will show members of one family buried near to each other, with in-laws, and connecting families all buried in the same churchyard or cemetery.

The information on a tombstone can be the bare facts such as 'John Henry Smith 1820–1888', which is not particularly helpful, but many families purchased plots and several members of one family may be buried together, their tombstone providing names, dates and relationships, added as each person died, such as:

John Henry Smith
born in this parish 1820
died of a chill 29 January 1888
beloved husband of Mary Ann
also
Mary Ann Smith
born in the parish of Asprey 1825
daughter of George and Katherine Howes
beloved mother of Henry Smith and Alice Green
who died 10 June 1898 aged 73 years
also
Alice Green
daughter of John Henry and Mary Anne Smith
wife of Daniel Green
died 21 April 1900 aged 55 years.

An MI with this amount of information can be of great help to a family historian, possibly giving details of members of the family not previously identified, or confirming information previously uncertain.

10

THE NATIONAL ARCHIVES

The main repository for the public records of England and Wales, and the United Kingdom, is situated at Ruskin Avenue, Kew. Formerly known as the Public Record Office (PRO), it merged with the Historical Manuscripts Commission (HMC) in April 2003 to form a new organization called The National Archives (TNA).

Although many famous documents are often on view in the Education and Visitor Centre at Kew, such as the Domesday Book, Shakespeare's will and the log book of HMS *Victory*, those most likely to be of interest to you are the documents that probably won't be on view, those that record events (such as divorces and court cases) in the lives of ordinary people, such as soldiers and sailors, civil servants, bankrupts, clergymen, criminals, emigrants and many more. Additional documentation held in the archives relates to government department records, including the Home, Foreign and War Offices, and maps and plans.

New information and documents are constantly becoming available. Kew's website is regularly updated to give details of new and forthcoming exhibitions, documents and information.

The archives are a short distance from both the underground and mainline stations, have ample parking space and are also served by several bus routes.

If you wish to engage in research there, it is necessary to obtain a reader's ticket at the Reception Desk at Kew. Existing but expired tickets can also be renewed here. No charge is made for a reader's ticket which will be issued to you on production of formal proof of your identity (such as a driver's licence, passport or bank card) and proof of your address (such as utility bill or bank statement). The reader's ticket is now a photocard so your photograph will also be taken on your first visit. You can pre-register in advance for a reader's ticket (up to four weeks before your visit) on the internet.

The times of opening are shown in the Appendix, but it is always worth a telephone call or checking the website to ensure that no changes have been made and also to enquire whether the records you wish to see are at Kew. The archives usually close for a week at the beginning of December for stocktaking, making a check at that time of the year essential.

On your first visit to Kew, you will also need to go on a brief tour which will introduce you to all the facilities and guide you on the best way to handle fragile documents. So allow enough time for this. To familiarize yourself in advance of your visit, you can take a virtual tour of the Archives on their website.

The rule of using only a pencil applies in all areas at Kew, and there are restrictions on the size and type of notepads and paper you can use. Check the website before you visit so that you know exactly what you can and cannot take with you into the Archives.

Readers are requested to take care of any fragile documents entrusted to them and not to put their notebooks on top of the documents nor to trace from them. Readers are allowed to request up to three documents at a time and there is no limit set on the time you may keep the documents. A request in advance for documents to be available on a certain day can be made by telephone, by email or by letter. This is particularly helpful if you know what documents you will require as it saves waiting time, which can be up to 30 minutes. A photocopying service is available and a leaflet gives the details of the charges for this.

Allow a whole day for your visit to Kew. In most cases you will find that your one day will extend to many others. The main reading room is on the first floor, with a smaller room for maps and large documents on the second floor. The Enquiry Desk, your first port of call, is in the Reference Room which also houses indexes, lists and reference books. There is a self-service restaurant and drink vending machines on the premises. No food or drink may be consumed in the reading rooms.

There is also a resource centre and reference library at Kew open to anyone with a reader's ticket. The library contains approximately 65,000 books, pamphlets, annuals, calendars and periodicals, plus a collection of CD-Roms. You can search the library catalogue online. A self-service photocopier is available and the library has quiet study areas (where there are sockets for laptop computers). There is also an Enquiries Desk for readers who need help.

There are many leaflets available giving details of the records held at Kew. You can also access these on the website. The staff at Kew are very helpful and will advise what records exist, how the coded reference system works and how to obtain documents for research. They cannot, however, assist with personal research. It is not possible in this book to give an indication of all the records available but the online Catalogue, formerly called PROCAT, contains details of what is held at Kew and lists over ten million separate documents. You can search it to find out the references of documents you are interested in, then order these online before your visit.

Divorce
Some case files for divorces which have taken place since 11 January 1858 are held at Kew although very few survive from 1938 onwards and those that do are subject to 30-year closure.

Case files are now destroyed 20 years after the divorce. Divorce cases where the Official Solicitor or the King's or Queen's Proctor was involved are subject to 75-year closure or longer.

Soldiers, Sailors and Airmen

Almost everyone has somebody in the family who became a member of the armed forces, whether a Cavalier or Roundhead in the Civil War of 1642–1649, a regular soldier serving in the South African War or a Royal Marine serving in the Second World War.

The War Office records held in the archives are by no means complete, but they are extensive. Some of the records are now available on the internet. There was no regular army in England before the Civil War. Earls, barons and kings raised armies as their needs dictated and no formal records were kept. Any records that were kept were in the hands of the regiments raised which were usually named after their colonels. There are some records relating to the armies of the Civil War with regiments listed together with their officers.

More and better service records were maintained after 1660 and many are available for research at Kew, both for officers and other ranks. Applications for pensions by army widows may give full names, addresses, dates of birth and marriage and names of children. Birthplaces of soldiers can also be found in Casualty Returns, Description Books and Pension Lists. Details of marriages and children are to be seen in Muster Rolls, Discharge Certificates and Regimental Pay Lists. If you are looking for an ancestor who served in any regiment, search the indexes of available material, or tell an attendant what you are looking for. He or she will be able to direct you to the correct documents.

Most of the service and pension records of the soldiers who served in the First World War were destroyed by enemy bombing in the Second World War. However, the records that survived the bombing, nicknamed the 'burnt documents', have been microfilmed and can be seen at Kew. They have also been scanned and digitized and are being made available on the Ancestry website. You can search the name index for free, and view the actual images by pay-by-view or subscription. These records contain information which is of great interest to family historians: for example, attestation papers (which give date of birth, next of kin, details of family members and address), discharge papers, medical records and casualty forms. It is estimated that you have a 40 per cent chance of finding the service records of a particular soldier.

The medal index cards for servicemen who served in the First World War can also be accessed at Kew. They have been digitized and made available via DocumentsOnline on The National Archives website so that you can search the records and, for a fee, download the record card you wish to see. You can also download scans of the cards from the Ancestry website (by pay-by-view or subscription). However, the Ancestry scans are in colour which makes them easier to read, and they also contain the backs of the cards which are not available on the TNA website. Not all the cards have any details written on the backs but those that do may contain useful information such as the address of the next of kin.

The Admiralty and Navy Board records at Kew are as detailed and extensive as those for the Army. They relate to Commissioned Officers, Warrant Officers, Ratings and Coastguards, covering all aspects of their service. Various documents giving names, places of birth, ages, and family details are available, such as Continuous Service Engagement Books for the years 1853–1872, Ships' Pay Books, Bounty Papers and Records of Officers' Services. Here again the staff will be able to advise you of the reference numbers and where to look if you are able to give them some information such as dates, or names of ships.

Through DocumentsOnline on the TNA website, you can

search and download the service records of more than 500,000 seamen who served in the Royal Navy between 1853 and 1923, as well as the records of the 50,000 officers and men who served in the Royal Naval Division between 1914 and 1919. On the Ancestry website you can search the records of the Royal Naval Division Casualties of the Great War.

In addition to naval records at Kew there are separate records for the Royal Marines covering service records of officers and other ranks. There are records of the Marine Pay Office, Letter and Description Books, all giving details of interest to the family historian.

Air Ministry records relating to personnel are not so extensive, relating mostly to operational records which do sometimes refer to specific men and women in the service.

The National Archives also holds information about prisoners of war from both the First and Second World Wars. This includes the liberation questionnaires that some Second World War ex-POWs completed on their release. Through DocumentsOnline you can search and download First World War interviews and reports for over 3,000 named ex-POWs.

Wills and Probate

As explained on page 108, wills prior to 1858 were dealt with by ecclesiastical or church courts, mainly the Prerogative Court of Canterbury (PCC) or the Prerogative Court of York (PCY). Where each will was dealt with depended on the date of death and the size of the estate of the deceased.

After 1769 a Legacy Duty became payable on a grant of probate and the Legacy Duty Registers are available at Kew. These Registers, which are unfortunately closed to the public for 125 years from the date the duty was entered in the Register, state in which court the probate was granted. Through DocumentsOnline you can search the Death Duty Registers for 1796 to 1811.

There are also records of litigation relating to wills and inventories of goods listed in wills. A preliminary search of the indexes relating to wills and probate will give some idea of the material available.

Some probate records are held at Kew where original documents can be seen. It is necessary to give three days' notice that you will require to see them. Court proceedings relating to disputed estates, which include plaintiff's statements and defendants' answers, can be seen at Kew.

Emigrants and Immigrants

There is no complete index of the names of foreigners entering England for the purpose of immigration, but there are many records in the archives. There are documents relating to alien clergymen, strangers in London, and documents from German, Swiss, French and Dutch churches. There are also Treasury records, Certificates of Aliens, Lists of Immigrants made by Ships' Masters, and Registers of Passenger Lists. On DocumentsOnline you can search and download the alien registration cards for the London area for the period 1876 to 1991.

Those leaving England to emigrate are also well represented in the records of the Colonial Office, the Home Office, the Board of Trade and the Treasury. There are lists of criminals deported to America and army pensioners who emigrated to Australia and New Zealand. If your researches lead you to think that one of your ancestors emigrated, it may take you a long time, but you could find him or her somewhere in the records at Kew or on the internet as more and more documents are made available online.

On the FindMyPast and AncestorsOnboard websites you can search and download (by pay-by-view or subscription) the passenger lists of those leaving the UK between 1890 and 1960. If you know the name of someone who emigrated, you can find the name of the ship and where they went. Whole families are often found together on one ship, also parties of orphans sent to Canada and Australia. Currently 16 million names can be searched. You can access the AncestorsOnboard website free of charge at Kew.

Also on FindMyPast you can search and download the register of passport applications between 1851 and 1903.

Unclaimed Money

You may have heard stories from your relatives of money due to the family but lost because of lack of evidence, or because 'Uncle George married again and we never found out what happened to the money'. The stories are various and inventive. There is a department of the Chancery Court that since 1876 has dealt with money deposited by solicitors who were unable to trace the next of kin or bene-ficiaries of an estate. If you can provide evidence of bene-ficial interest, the details of such accounts can be inspected free of charge. There are also lists published by the *London Gazette* which can be seen at Kew and on the Gazettes website. It may be worth a try if you think your family story is founded on facts which you have substantiated by your researches.

The Police

Certain documentation relating to the Metropolitan Police is available at Kew, such as certificates of service from 1889–1909 and registers giving names of those who joined the police and those who left between 1829–1947. If you have a family tradition of fathers and sons joining the police force, you may be able to trace several generations using these records. You may also find some useful information online at the Police Orders and Met Police websites.

The Post Office
The records of the Post Office are public records but are not held at Kew. They are held at the British Postal Museum and Archives in London (see Appendix). Amongst other items they hold Treasury Letter Books, Monthly Cash Books, Salary Lists (from 1635), Establishment Books (from 1742) and Appointment Books from 1831. The oldest item is a Household Book of Queen Anne dated 1702.

There are many other categories of records in the archives available to you, to help you trace your ancestors, including Change of Name deeds, Shipping records, Private Conveyances or Sales of Land, Manorial Court Rolls and maps, Apprenticeship records, Railway Companies before nationalization to name but a few. They are all there waiting for you. All you need is time, patience and perseverance.

If you live locally, it may be worthwhile to pay a short visit to Kew to collect as much literature as is available giving details of all the records and familiarize yourself with the layout of the building. At the same time, you can obtain a reader's ticket and possibly spend a little time finding out how to use the computer ordering system. When you have sifted through information in the leaflets, make a list of any of the records that you think might assist you and then spend a full day, using all your time there to best advantage by preparing thoroughly for your visit before you go.

Alternatively, you may prefer to search the website and download the information leaflets which relate to your particular interests. Again, find out as much as possible before your visit so that you use your actual research time at Kew as profitably as you can.

11

MORE SOURCES
FOR RESEARCH

Now that you are beginning to build a picture of your family history, where else can you look to help you? There are many other sources of information available to you to assist in your search for your living relatives and your ancestors. Even the most experienced family historian or genealogist can get lost and does not always know where to look. Always be ready to listen and take advice. Family historians can be helpful to each other.

When you do find a new source, keep a note of the address and telephone number in your Information Book with an indication of what records are available, the times of opening and any fees charged. Make a note of the name of someone who has been particularly helpful. Keep your Information Book up to date when you learn of any changes. You may be able to help someone else with that information.

The Internet
There is a vast amount of help available on the internet, including websites where experts offer guidance, where societies answer questions, and where libraries and archives

give information. There are so many guides and finding aids that it would be impossible to list them all here. However, when you find a website that you think may be useful in the future, enter its address into your 'favorites' or 'bookmarks' folder or make a note in your manual notebook.

When you are looking for a particular subject of interest, simply type the relevant word into your chosen search engine and it will find all the sites containing that word. Often the number of pages offered is so overwhelming that it's a good idea to follow the advice offered by your search engine on how to focus the search as closely as you can on your specific topic.

There are many websites maintained by volunteers who charge no fee for their assistance and a great number of knowledgeable people on the web wanting to help. Some of the sites are regularly updated but others may not be. It is a good idea, therefore, to look at the end of a page where the last time a site is updated is usually given.

One of the best family history sites is 'Cyndi's List'. This is well-known and contains a great deal of information relating to genealogy worldwide.

Another very useful website is GENUKI which has a mass of information for family history researchers.

Many record archives, libraries and museums have email and their staff will usually be happy to answer your questions directly by email. Most of them reply very promptly and give very detailed information. If you wish to email a repository and don't know its electronic address, type the name into your search engine to find its website which should show its email address.

Alternatively, you can use a registry of repositories such as ARCHON. This directory on The National Archives website gives information on all repositories in the United Kingdom and worldwide which hold collections of manuscripts which are noted in the indexes to the National Register of Archives.

The Access to Archives website is also very useful. It

enables you to search the catalogues of around 400 repositories in England and Wales, including local record offices, libraries, universities, museums, and national and specialist institutions. You can search to see what records mention your particular family name or cover the town or village where they originated. The website is frequently updated as more and more records are incorporated into their catalogue.

If you have relations who were killed in action during the First or Second World Wars, the Commonwealth War Graves Commission website is worth visiting. Here you can search the Debt of Honour Register for the whereabouts of their graves or the monuments where their names are commemorated. In some cases, additional information (such as names of next of kin and their addresses) is also included.

Saga's website includes a program named 'Circles' in which people leave their names stating the subjects in which they are interested. There is a genealogy page where you can leave your own name and look for others who are interested in the subject.

Telephone Directories

Have you tried telephone directories? You have probably at some time seen your surname in telephone directories and wondered whether there is any relationship to yourself. If you have an uncommon name, once again you are lucky, there will not be so many to choose from. When you have found some addresses from the certificates you have obtained, look through the telephone directories of those areas. Your local library may have a collection of telephone directories in its reference department, either for the present day relating to other areas or old directories relating to your own area. If they do not, they may be able to tell you where you can see them. Alternatively, run a search on the directory enquiry telephone listings available on the internet. Or search the British Phone Book database on the Ancestry website.

You may be surprised to find that people with the same family name are still living at the address given in your certificates. If they are, try phoning them, they can only say no, but they may say yes and another door will open. It would have to be quite a coincidence if they were not a branch of the same family. Alternatively, write to people with the same surname telling them you are working on your family history. Give them a few details of your family and ask if they are a branch of your family. Send a stamped addressed envelope for their reply. Be careful in your approach by letter and telephone. Make sure that you establish a definite relationship, by discussing other relatives, before you make any form of personal contact.

Television and Radio Programmes
Watch out for factual television and radio programmes, particularly those in your local region, relating in detail historical incidents or events concerning the lives of famous people and places. There have been very interesting and informative programmes about the building of railways, war episodes, village life, church buildings, financial institutions, famous hospitals, children in Victorian times, statesmen, soldiers, and many other subjects. These programmes are often well researched and factually correct. They may throw some light on a subject of interest to you as a family historian, giving you some ideas for sources of research that you had not previously considered. Those about places directly of interest to your family can be very helpful, even if they relate to today. Interviews with local characters on regional programmes can provide odd items of interest, opening up more areas for research.

Early black and white films especially those made in

England can show places and buildings long demolished but about which somewhere there must be some written information.

TV programmes, such as *The History Detectives*, (produced in association with The Open University) and, of course, *Who Do You Think You Are?*, can be helpful, as can radio programmes such as Radio 4's *Tracing Your Roots* and *Making History*. However, it must be remembered that television programmes are made as entertainment and are able to spend a great deal of money, whisking celebrities off to India, Eastern Europe and other countries. They also sometimes are able to gain access to original documents which are not available to ordinary people and viewers don't see the hours of research that go into the making these programmes. So don't be disappointed if you are unable to emulate them.

Directories

Street and trade directories can give invaluable assistance in tracing members of your family. These can also be found in local reference libraries and county record offices.

If you are searching to establish an address in the City of London or a London Borough, the Guildhall Reference Library in the City of London has an extensive collection of street and trade directories commencing as early as the middle of the 18th century. Their collection also extends beyond the London area, covering many parts of the country. The Guildhall has much to offer the family history researcher and genealogist which I refer to specifically in the next chapter.

Most areas, rural and urban, published directories, and families, particularly those in business, or tradespeople, can be traced through many years in those directories. Directories are also useful if you wish to trace roads or streets. If you find a reference to a family name at a given address in an early directory, you can check that address in the census returns. If your family appears, you will once again have a grouping and not just one person.

Approaching the problem the other way, if a census return has given the occupations of members of the family, there may be a trade directory relating to their trade or occupation where their names appear with details of what they did.

Anyone connected with a bank or merchant house would probably appear in the Bankers Almanac, another kind of trade directory. Well known directories covering a wider area are Kelly's, White's and the Post Office directories. Some commence as early as 1750 and continue through to the 1950s.

Local directories often give a short history of the surrounding area, mentioning places of special interest, churches, schools, inns, public houses, institutions, working men's clubs, hospitals and workhouses. People mentioned by name will be local gentry, publicans, schoolmasters, town officials and clergymen. Trade and street directories are a rich source of information.

Some directories are available on CD from commercial organizations and family history societies. At the time of writing, the University of Leicester's historical directories website (providing a digital library of local and trade directories for England and Wales from 1750 to 1919) is still available on the internet, although as funding for the project has ended no new material is being added to the site.

Newspapers and Magazines

Newspaper, periodical and magazine archives are another area for research which should not be overlooked, containing, as they do, news and stories relating to family life. Newspapers were first published early in the 17th century and offer much to the family historian in the way of historical happenings, including names of people and places and pictures. Even the advertisements can tell you something. There are many collections of newspapers both local and national. Some are held on microfilm, others hold the original newspapers bound into volumes. Ask at your local library where you can see newspaper archives. Try your local newspaper, if you have one. They will probably have copies of their own publications. Early newspapers may be available at your local reference library or county record office.

The Guildhall Library in the City of London has a complete collection of *The Times* newspaper on microfilm. It also has copies of the *London Gazette*. As mentioned on page 122, there is a Gazettes website. *The Times* from 1785 to 1985 has also been digitized and is available through participating libraries through a digital database. Ask at your local library or check their website to see whether it is available.

As well as local record offices and libraries there is a vast library of national, provincial and overseas newspapers and periodicals held in the British Library Newspaper Library in Colindale, London. You will need a Newspaper Library reader's pass or a British Library photographic reader's pass to visit the library. (See page 145 for more information.) The Bodleian Library in Oxford also has a collection of newspapers and you will also need a reader's pass to visit this institution.

How can newspapers help you? Announcements of births, marriages, divorces and deaths appear in the personal columns. If you have a birth or death certificate search the personal columns near the dates. A birth will give the names of the parents and possibly an address. A death notice often gives the names of several members of the family together with information concerning the burial which might lead you to the churchyard and a memorial stone. A death notice may give an indication of an inquest which could be followed up. Engagement and marriage announcements can also be informative, giving the names of the parents of the intended bride and groom. If one of the parents is a widow or widower the marriage announcement usually gives that information. Photographs of weddings often appear in local newspapers accompanied by descriptions of the occasion, giving names of those present at the reception. On their deaths obituaries of local gentry and other prominent people appear. Details of fatal accidents appear which might finally dispel the family story of how 'Great Uncle George died'. Details of court cases are given and reports of many local happenings which may have affected members of your family. Strikes, house fires, floods, murders, all are chronicled somewhere in newspapers. Look through the notes you have made from the information given to you by members of your family. If there is a particular item of interest with a 'near enough' date, look for it in the newspapers around that date. You may find full details and a photograph. Not all the stories you read in the newspapers will be completely factual, but they may be able to confirm in more detail some family stories that you have already obtained. We have to remember that they were written for the reader from a journalistic point of view with the aim of selling as many copies as possible. Headlines in particular can be very misleading. In many cases it will be possible to obtain photocopies of the items you are seeking which you can add to your supporting documentation. Advertisements can also be a source of information: notices of auctions, houses for sale, etc., often give the name of the vendor, shopkeepers, and tradesmen offering services. From about 1840 shipping companies offered sailings to Australia and America, giving details of the names of ships, dates of sailings and the cost. Theatrical productions are also advertised giving the names of the performers. If one of your forebears was a travelling player you might follow his progress through newspaper advertisements – 'Direct from the Palace Theatre London' or 'Next week at Scarborough'.

If you do not find any reference to your family in early newspapers, it is still worthwhile looking through them for the places where they lived. It will help you to form a general picture of their lives, the clothes they wore, the houses they lived in, the work they did, their leisure pursuits, the illnesses and disasters they suffered as seen through the contemporary reports.

County Record Offices
Many counties in England and Wales have a record office, created in an effort to preserve and gather together local records and documents. There are also record offices in some of the London Boroughs and one in Edinburgh. They house original parish records, wills, court records, civil records, family archives, manorial documents and many other documents relating to local affairs which have been deposited with them. Some counties have several record offices, some only one. Each record office has its own rules and regulations, days of closing, and hours of opening. Some of the documents may be available on microfilm only. Before making your journey to the record office, check their website or make a telephone call to enquire whether you need to reserve a microfilm machine or make an appointment. This will save time for both you and the archivist. In most record offices the rules about not eating or drinking while carrying out research on original documents and the use of pencils only for making notes apply. Make a list of what you are looking for. This will also save time and will assist the archivist who will help you by providing the films or documentation you are seeking. If he is told of your particular interest in a simple manner he will know where to look for the documents which will be most useful to you. The staff in the record offices have expert knowledge of the documents in their care and are usually very helpful. You may have to wait a little time while those documents are being found but there will be open library shelves with directories, street maps and books of local interest which may offer sources for research while you wait.

There may be a limit to the number of documents you can have for your use at one time, so return a document as soon as you have made your notes and finished with it. Photocopies and copy certificates are obtainable on payment of fixed fees. Take enough money with you to cover these charges, particularly small change since you may need it if you are able to make your own photocopies by putting coins in a machine.

The International Genealogical Index

The Genealogical Society of the Church of the Latter-day Saints (LDS) in Salt Lake City, Utah, USA, is compiling an index of worldwide baptisms and marriages, known as the IGI. The reason for this dedicated undertaking, which by its very nature can never be finished, is that according to Mormon beliefs they can baptise their ancestors into their faith. Whatever their reasons, their work is greatly appreciated by family historians and genealogists. The IGI is a vast area for research, believed to record over 80 million entries and growing all the time. It is based on the computer records held in Utah. The records are taken from pre-civil registration vital records and church records and relate to persons no longer living, the earliest entry being for the year 1538.

Microfiche copies of the 1988 and 1992 edition of the index are available and have been purchased by many outlets and can be seen at Kew, county record offices, reference libraries, family history societies and the Society of Genealogists. The latest edition of the index, for 1993 with 1997 addenda, is on a CD-Rom which is also available at different venues. As you may need to reserve a microfiche machine or computer in order to access the IGI, contact the venue before you visit.

The microfiche index is chronological and alphabetical by surname with the first names also given in alphabetical order, county by county and parish by parish within each county for England and Scotland. Wales and Ireland are each shown as a

single unit without counties. It is not a complete record of each
county, some counties having better coverage than others. On
each microfiche is a list of its contents which should be
consulted first to check that you have the correct film and to find
out whether the parish you require has been recorded. It is also
possible to obtain these lists in printed form from a London
research agency, the Mormon Church having given permission
for the reprint. The series is not published in order of counties as
on the microfiche, but in volumes of geographical areas. These
listings also have a very good introduction and explanation of
how best to use the IGI indexes.

The information given in the IGI in relation to a baptism is
the name of the person, the date, the names of the parents and
the parish where the baptism took place. Marriages show the
names of both parties, which are cross referenced, the date and
the parish. Not all the information is gathered from parish
records. There is a column headed 'Type' which shows which
event is recorded or where the information was obtained.
Initial letters are used as follows:

A = Adult christening
B = Birth
C = Christening
D = Death or Burial
M = Marriage
N = Census
S = Miscellaneous
W = Will or Probate
F = Birth or christening of first known child

Instruction on how to read, interpret and evaluate the information contained in the IGI, both positive and negative, is
deserving of a chapter of its own. The IGI contains an
immense amount of data. However, it must be emphasized
that the IGI is only an aid to your research, it does have many

errors and omissions and any information gained must be checked against the original records.

You can search the IGI on the internet on the LDS's Family Search website. There you can also search the Ancestral File. This is a computerized database of genealogies submitted to the LDS by people from all over the world.

The LDS are working on digitizing and putting on the internet much or most of the film in their archives. This is a massive operation, currently in the early stages.

If you live near an LDS family history centre it is well worth visiting it to carry out research. The Church has microfilm and microfiche copies of a vast range of genealogical records, including census returns, parish registers and probate records, and you can gain access to these at all LDS family history centres for a fee.

Family History Fairs
Family history fairs are very popular and held in many places. They are usually advertised in magazines and local newspapers, including the annual fair of the Society of Genealogists.

Teletext
On Channel 4's Teletext, there are a number of pages named 'Family Tree'. Currently starting on page 174/175 there are enquiries from researchers seeking help with their family history. At present there are enquiries from England, Scotland, Canada and Wales. The entries are changed every Monday. Enquirers are asked to send in their queries, which should be no longer than 50 words. The address for queries is shown in the Appendix. 'Family Tree' can also be viewed on Sky and Freeview, and on the Teletext website.

There are also pages for people researching Service personnel at 172 and a page named 'Lost Touch' at page 171.

Military Service Records

Comprehensive military service records for family members after 1922 can be obtained directly from the Records Department, Ministry of Defence (see Appendix). Give the name of the person you are researching and any information you have, such as regiment, ship or place of service. You will have to establish your relationship to that person and will probably have to pay a fee.

12

LIBRARIES AND RESEARCH CENTRES

Most librarians and archivists are helpful people, willing to devote their time and interest if you approach them in a sensible and friendly manner. Their time is precious and many people seek their assistance. Polite requests for help and an indication that you are willing to wait will usually achieve better results than demands for instant attention. Make your requests as short as possible, but give as much information as you have. They do not usually have time to hear the whole history of one of your ancestors, leading up to a simple question, much as they may wish to. If you know dates or places, write them down and give them to the librarian so that he can take the information with him when looking for documents for you. There are many places where you can carry out your own research once you have obtained a little help and a nudge in the right direction from an expert.

The Society of Genealogists

The Society of Genealogists (see Appendix) was founded in London in 1911 and was granted a Coat of Arms in 1986 to mark the 75th anniversary of its foundation. Its members are professional genealogists, amateur family historians and anyone interested in family history research. Its headquarters were in Harrington Gardens but due to expansion of its ever growing library it moved to Charterhouse Buildings in the City of London, which was once a silk warehouse, making access easier and its proximity to the other major research centres an advantage for its members. The Society is a non-profit-making registered charity whose objects are to promote and encourage the study of genealogy. Anyone interested in genealogy and family history research can apply to become a member and pay the yearly subscription. Non-members may use the library facilities of the Society on payment of search fees, by the hour, half day or by the day.

The Society issues a quarterly magazine free to its members, holds meetings and runs classes on many subjects that fall within the realm of genealogy. Introductory Saturday mornings are run for new members, giving an extensive tour of the library with instruction on how to use the facilities. The Society also runs courses on the use of computers and the internet for family history researchers. The Society of Genealogists claims that its library is unique in England and that no other library can offer such extensive research facilities for the family historian. Almost all the books are on open shelves, giving researchers immediate access so that time is not wasted waiting for books to be brought by attendants. In addition, borrowing facilities are available to members by mail, upon payment by the member of the mailing charges. The books on the shelves are arranged alphabetically by county with a separate section for countries and relate to all aspects of family history. There are local history books, poll books, directories, county records, genealogical periodicals and magazines. Details of the Monumental Inscriptions that have been copied and indexed are available filed under each county, as are books and information relating to minority religions. Most of the material held relates to the period before registration (1837) which makes it all the more useful.

In addition to printed books, the Society holds a large

collection of manuscripts and typescripts deposited with it by private persons, including family histories. These are available in boxes on closed access in the Lower Library and are produced on request. The Society holds a large collection of parish register copies, the largest in the country, in printed, typescript and manuscript form, dating from as early as 1538 through to 1812 and some through to 1837. All are listed in the library catalogue. If you are unable to find the one you wish to see, ask the library attendants, since some of the unbound copies are not on the open shelves. Boyd's Marriage Index, a collection of over 500 volumes indexing marriages between 1538 and 1837, is held by the Society. It covers many counties of England (not Wales or Scotland) and some counties have separate indexes for males and females. Boyd's gives information relating to dates and places of marriages indicating the parish register in which more detailed information can be traced.

Indexes of early marriage licences, wills and apprenticeship records are available. These are particularly useful since you can search them while on a visit to the Society and decide whether a trip to other repositories such as Kew or a county record office to inspect the original documents would prove useful.

The IGI on microfiche, covering the whole of the world, is available at the Society. If you wish to search the IGI it is not necessary to telephone or write in advance to reserve the use of a microfiche machine. A copying service is available on payment of a small fee per page.

Many trade directories are on the library shelves, filed alphabetically under the counties. There are London directories starting as early as 1677 and a collection of Dublin directories covering ninety years from 1761.

Other subjects covered are schools and universities with an extensive collection of registers, also directories and registries of professions including law lists of solicitors and barristers, clergymen, doctors and surgeons, judges, architects, musicians and many more.

As you will appreciate, there is a wealth of information to be gained from a visit to the Society of Genealogists. By using the library, in one day you might possibly save yourself several separate visits to more distant research repositories or could at least form some idea of whether a visit would prove fruitful. The library, which is closed on Mondays, is open on other days for as many as eight hours giving you the advantage of a good long day for research. In order to make the best use of the Society's library, make a list of all the names or subjects you wish to research and follow it closely. You may be tempted, but unless you have a spare day on which to indulge yourself, do not dip into books that attract your attention or you will be side-tracked and not look for all you are seeking, as I know to my cost. The Society's library is an Aladdin's Cave of genealogical and historical data.

The library is arranged on three floors. Researchers are requested not to take bags and briefcases into the reading rooms and a cloakroom with lockers is provided on the ground floor.

The entrance is on the ground floor. The Society publishes many books and finding aids, which can be purchased at the reception desk. They are also available by mail or through the internet.

Entrance to all floors is gained by use of a swipe card system. Detailed 'floor guides' are shown on each floor and can be obtained free of charge before your visit if required. Printed handouts are also available to assist you to use the computerized catalogue. There are enquiry desks on each floor and computer terminals giving access to the catalogue which shows how to find the items held by the Society, their reference numbers and their location. If 'Apply to Library Staff' applies to an item, it will be produced for you in the Lower Library on request.

On the ground floor is the cloakroom and locker room, as

well as a lecture hall (with a loop system for those using hearing aids), a common room with comfortable chairs and a drinks vending machine. Toilet facilities for the disabled are also provided on this floor. There is a lift to all floors and access for disabled researchers.

The Lower Library, which is in the basement, houses a research centre containing film and fiche readers, and a large number of computers with free access to various databases.

The Middle Library houses the Society's collection of textbooks and their printed collections for the British Isles arranged by county.

The Upper Library houses the printed collection for overseas with a special section for professions, schools and the armed forces.

A magazine *Computers in Genealogy*, which gives advice, current information and reviews on software, is published for the Society.

The Society holds a number of open days each year for members and non-members. Visitors are given a tour of the library and demonstrations of the available technology.

SOGCAT (the Society of Genealogist's library catalogue) is now accessible online. It contains details of everything that is in the library except the Documents Collection. Some of the Society's databases, including Boyd's Marriage Index, the Marriage Licence Allegations Index and the Apprentices of Great Britain database, are also available on the British Origins website. Society members can view all the Society's material on the site and are awarded one 72-hour British Origins session per calendar quarter (unlimited searches over 72 consecutive hours).

Guildhall Library
The Guildhall Library in London (see Appendix) has a department devoted to genealogy, covering in detail the City of

London, London Boroughs and the Greater London area together with information relating to other counties. There are no search fees, all that is required is a signature in the visitors' book at the enquiry desk in the manuscript room. There is usually an attendant on duty just inside the entrance to the library who will direct you to the manuscript room which is up a small flight of stairs to the left through the map room. To the right is the reference library.

The manuscript room and library have a plentiful supply of desks and comfortable chairs for the use of readers. The manuscript room, which has both microfilm and microfiche machines, has a collection on microfilm of the parish registers of the City of London, the London Boroughs, parts of Greater London and the County of Middlesex. They also have the microfiche of the IGI covering the same areas. The microfiche for the British Isles are held in the library where there are several microfiche and microfilm machines available for use and it is not necessary to make an appointment. There are also copies of census records in the reference library. This is particularly helpful since you do not have to wait for the films to be brought to you, but can help yourself, and view them on the microfilm machines in the library room. Copying facilities are also available (again small change necessary).

There are extensive records relating to the City of London, including City institutions such as the famous Goldsmiths and Silversmiths, together with other less well known Guilds and Livery Companies with apprenticeship records, such as the Clock and Watchmakers and the Fishmongers. If you have an ancestor who was a tradesman or craftsman in the City of London these records are very helpful. There are Law Lists from 1797, records of the Royal College of Surgeons of England from 1518. There are records relating to the House of Commons, Old Bailey trials, naturalization papers and Change of Name deeds.

Books on the shelves of the reference library cover a wide

range. One of the largest collections of trade and street directories in the country is held by this library. Some are on open shelves, some are locked behind glass fronted shelves and others are kept elsewhere on the premises. If you do not see the directories you require, ask at the desk where there are several archivists and librarians available to assist you. Tell them the number of the table where you are sitting and complete an application form and the books will be brought to you. There is a large card index of all the books and manuscripts available and if anything you wish to see is not readily available, ask at the desk. The archivists and librarians are very knowledgeable about the books on their shelves and very willing to help with problems. If they do not have the information on their own shelves, they will probably be able to direct you to another library or repository where you can find the information you are seeking.

In addition the reference library holds on microfilm a complete run of *The Times* newspaper.

London Metropolitan Archives

The London Metropolitan Archives (see Appendix) contain a wealth of information which is of interest to people with ancestors in London. It has been updated and renovated with digitized indexes to the records. They plan to put their entire catalogue online and to operate an online ordering system, starting with the parish registers.

The City of London's London Signatures website currently includes an index of 10,000 wills from the Archdeaconry Court of Middlesex as well as 23,500 marriage bonds from the Commissary for the Archdeaconry of Surrey. You can search these free online and buy a digital copy of any will or marriage bond from the website.

Federation of Family History Societies

There are many family history societies throughout the country which come under the umbrella of the Federation (including sixteen family history societies covering most of Scotland). Every county has at least one. Most local societies concentrate on family history research within their own county and produce a regular journal relating to their work. If your research takes you outside the county in which you now live, write to or email the secretary of the society in the county you wish to research, giving the surname or place names in which you are interested. The local society may have someone amongst it who has been researching that name or can tell you about the place. If you join your own local society, it will exchange information through the Federation with other societies. The Federation also publishes many useful booklets relating to different aspects of family history research.

An online partnership has been agreed between the FFHS and the FindMyPast website, whereby online data originally available on the FFHS's FamilyHistoryOnline website is transferred to FindMyPast's website.

There is also a Guild of One Name Studies (GOONS) affiliated to the Federation, specializing in the study of one name only. If there is a society for your name, or any of the family names that you are researching, their research and publications may be of interest to you although they may not necessarily have any information relating to your particular family even if the name is the same.

Borthwick Institute of Historical Research, York

The Borthwick Institute in St Anthony's Hall, York (see Appendix), is a research institute of York University and holds many original manuscripts which could help those in the north who do not have the time and money to make protracted journeys to London. They specialize in the study of church history, particularly in relation to administration and law in the northern province. The Institute is mainly for the use of research students, but it is open to the public. It is necessary to make an appointment in advance if you wish to carry out research on their archives. There is a room where readers can consume their own food and facilities for making tea and coffee supplied for a small charge. There is also a copying service available for some classes of documents.

The library known as the Gurney Library holds approximately 20,000 books on its shelves, relating to all aspects of historic research including local societies and most record offices. Copy parish registers, probate records and Bishops' Transcripts are held, as are original manuscripts and typescripts deposited by private families and individuals relating to Yorkshire and Nottinghamshire. Estate records, charity papers, school records, and wills are also available. It is advisable to enquire whether it holds the documentation you are seeking before embarking on an appointment to carry out research. The Institute publishes a helpful guide giving details of its genealogical sources which may be of assistance to family historians. The Institute specializes in document conservation and restoration and if you can take a tour of its work and conservation rooms I would urge you to do so. You will be privileged to see many famous early documents and manuscripts and the meticulous loving care and scientific research carried on by the 'backroom boys' at the Institute.

The Newspaper Library

The Newspaper Library at Colindale (see Appendix) is a branch of the British Library where you can research amongst nearly 600,000 volumes, and 220,000 microfilms housed on about 18 miles of shelving. Its stock is increased each year with up-to-date newspapers, but it is past newspapers that will interest you more. The library is easy to reach, being almost opposite Colindale underground station which is on the Northern line. There is also a very small car park.

Admission to the library is free. It is restricted to those over 18 years of age and it is necessary to obtain a reader's ticket by producing proof of identity. Before you visit, it is a good idea to search the Newspaper Library Web Catalogue which is available on the internet. However, the library also suggests that you telephone or email in advance of your visit, in order to ascertain that it does hold the information you require and, if so, to reserve it so that it is available on your arrival. (Some items are held off-site and you need to give 48 hours' notice.) When you ring, you can also check what proof of identity you will be asked to supply.

In the library there are over 150 seats for readers including more than 50 with microfilm machines. The online catalogue of all the newspapers and periodicals in the library can be accessed free of charge via computer terminals in the library.

There are photocopying facilities and copies can be supplied by post if you can give an exact reference of the piece you are seeking. There is a refreshment room with drinks and food vending machines where you can also eat your own food.

The newspaper collections dating from 1800 are daily and weekly papers and periodicals including London newspapers. Provincial, Welsh, Scottish and Irish newspapers are held dating from 1700 as well as foreign newspapers. There is also a collection of printed books relating to the newspaper industry, journalism and the history of the press.

For a fixed fee, the library staff will search newspapers on your behalf. Application forms are available on the internet.

The British Library plans to close the Colindale library by 2012 and move the newspaper collection to Boston Spa. Access to the newspaper library will then be provided by microfilm or digital copies at the main St Pancras British Library site.

The Oriental and India Office Collections

Many of us have ancestors who were connected with India, either through work or through the armed forces. Young men set out for India to make their fortunes by working for the British East India Company or joined regiments of the army which were based in India. There they married, had families and often died. Some fell in love with the country and on discharge from the army remained there to work on the railway. All those lives were well documented and the records are today held in the Oriental and India Office Collections of the British Library in Euston Road, London (see Appendix).

The Collections are found on the third floor of the British Library. You don't need special permission or to make an appointment to visit the OIOC Reading Room but you do need to have a valid British Library reader's pass which can be applied for at the Reader Admissions office. However, the OIOC strongly advises that anyone wishing to visit their Collections to make enquiries should write, fax, email or telephone in advance to check opening hours.

Bags, coats and umbrellas must not be taken into the Reading Room but left in lockers or in the cloakroom on the lower ground floor. There is a restaurant on the first floor and a café on the upper ground floor. The Reading Room has seats for 108 readers, including areas for microfilm readers and portable computer users. You may consult reference books from the open shelves at Reading Room desks but you need to request to see other books or documents by using the Online Catalogue terminals or, for some items, by filling in a requisition form available at the Issue Desk.

There are copying facilities available: there is a self-service reader-printer (for microfilm negatives) and a self-service photocopier (for printed materials only).

Leaflets on the Collections and how to use the OIOC's Reading Room are available on request. There are also more detailed guides to the Board of Control collection,

Ecclesiastical Returns and Sources for Family History Research.

The extensive records which are of most interest to the family historian are the ecclesiastical and army records giving details of births, marriages and deaths, service records both civil and military, wills, probate and pension funds. They cover the East India Company from 1600 to 1858, the Board of Control from 1784 to 1858, the India Office from 1858 to 1947 and the Burma Office from 1937 to 1948. The records cover much written material, that which was sent to India from England and that sent to England from India. They cover not only India, but parts of Burma, Indonesia, Malaysia, St Helena, China and Japan. An interesting item amongst the records of St Helena is the death certificate of Napoleon Bonaparte. Unfortunately in 1858 many records were disposed of as 'waste paper' and were sold to a dealer. Fortunately the dealer realized how important the 'waste paper' was and spent the next fifty years selling the records back to the India Office so all was not lost.

On the India Family website you can search 300,000 births, baptisms, marriages, deaths and burials from the Indian Office records. These relate mainly to Europeans in India, including medical staff, civil servants and military personnel.

Trade Museums and Libraries

There are very many museums and libraries devoted to one subject, tucked away in back streets, not necessarily in London but all over the country. If by tradition your family or ancestors specialized in a particular trade or interest, passing down their knowledge from father to son over the ages, there is probably a museum for you somewhere, where you might find specific reference to your family name. You may even find photographs amongst their archives. Most of the Guilds and Livery Halls in the City of London have museums. If your ancestors were stonemasons, or train drivers, worked in the potteries, were butchers, glass blowers, doctors, carpenters, or opera singers, there are collections of records looked after by devoted archivists somewhere waiting for you. It is well worth making enquiries. Your local library should have a copy of the 'Museum Year Book' which gives all the museums in the British Isles with addresses, telephone numbers and hours of opening or you can search on the internet.

There is a Mining Museum in Wakefield, a Bagpipe Museum in Morpeth and a Museum for Chartered Insurance in London (see Appendix) to give just three examples. Principal museums in cities and large towns mount special exhibitions from time to time. Watch out for announcements and articles in the local or national press. The subjects are varied, some local and some based on international events, but many are of interest to the family historian. St Paul's Cathedral in London had an exhibition of Jewish records in the crypt, showing many early photographs. The Print Library in a small back street near St Bride's in London (see Appendix) has a permanent collection related to all aspects of the paper trade, including the manufacture and printing of paper and books. I was directed to that particular library by a librarian at the Guildhall Library when I was researching someone connected with the paper trade. The archivist was very helpful and eventually found a collection of house magazines for the company where the person concerned had been an apprentice. In one of those little booklets I found a detailed written history giving his full name and date of birth, his father's name, their address at the signing of the indentures together with a history of his rise in the company's employment and details of his marriage and his children. A really wonderful find!

13

BOOK ONE OF YOUR
FAMILY HISTORY

One of the pleasures of tracing your family history is the fact that you can take a rest whenever you wish and return to it at any time. Some of those 'bitten by the bug' spend most of their leisure time working at their family history, often using their weekends and annual holidays to visit archives, record offices and registries or the places where their forebears originated. For those living in England whose forebears originated elsewhere, a visit to Ireland, Wales, Scotland or even further can combine a very pleasant holiday with an opportunity to continue the research. The Society of Genealogists and the Federation of Family History Societies offer interesting and valuable evening classes, weekend and week long seminars and conferences. A few days spent in the company of dedicated family historians and genealogists gives renewed energy and determination to continue. And what a lot you can learn in those few days! If you have become a member of the Society of Genealogists you will receive information of all lectures, seminars and conferences. If not, write at the beginning of the year to ask for its programme or check its website so that you can plan any trips you wish to make.

Once you have found addresses where your forebears lived and the locations of some of their burials, visit the places if you can, taking your camera or persuade a photographer friend to accompany you. Some of the houses and buildings mentioned in your documentation may have disappeared by now. In towns and cities whole streets of houses have been demolished to make way for modern redevelopment and country areas are now crisscrossed by motorways. You may be lucky, however and find the house where a great-great-grand-parent was born. I found one such house in a small town in Scotland. The male members of the family had been stone-masons through the ages and there was a carving over the front door of the house showing stonemasons' tools with the date 1720. I could picture George Thompson carefully carving that stone, little knowing how delighted one of his ancestors would be to find it 260 years later. A photograph of the house and the carving now form part of my documentation. I was also able to purchase a booklet, in a small local museum, giving the history of the area. All these things give depth and perspective to a family history. Visiting houses, towns and villages brings you closer to the people you are researching and makes you aware of the pleasures and difficulties of their lives.

Visiting churchyards and cemeteries can also bring pleasure as well as sadness. Branches of families die out or move away leaving gravestones neglected. The weather and time are very destructive, but a tranquil picture of a church-yard, a memorial stone standing under a tree and a close-up of that stone will add greatly to the narrative of a family history.

If you should get a little bored ploughing your way through the indexes, take a rest and turn to other things. You have your records to keep up to date, a good task to undertake in the winter months when the nights are longer and travelling is not so easy. Your family chart should be revised and updated as you delve further into the past. You also have the task of bringing all the information together on paper.

Not all of you will wish to write a book, but page by page your manuscript will grow. Once you have sufficient information start to write your family history. If using your computer, it can be downloaded and put into a loose-leaf ring binder, adding separate pages as you write. This will eventually combine with your family tree, photographs, original and copy documents. You can also keep them in chronological order, inserting them in the correct place without difficulty.

Although you are writing the story for yourself in order to bring together the results of your researches, it will undoubtedly be read by others. Members of your family will wish to read it and you may care to deposit a copy with the Society of Genealogists to assist the generations to come. Make it as interesting as you can. If you have the necessary information, describe what people looked like, the colour of their hair and eyes, how tall they were, together with a reference to any outstanding features. You will find that members of your family will sometimes be surprised by descriptions of their distant kinsmen and recognize in those descriptions likenesses to today's descendants.

Start by making notes of one person on the first page. Try using yourself as the first person. What do you know? Your name – put that at the top of the page. On this page, which is a guide for yourself on which to base the final manuscript, add your reference numbers so that you can refer to your records. The final manuscript does not need to show the reference numbers since they will become a distraction to anyone reading the family history. On each line underneath, add another piece of information, date of birth, place of birth, parents' names, schools attended, examinations passed, degrees won, interests and unusual hobbies, residences occupied with the dates of the moves. If you are married, the date and place of your marriage, the name of your spouse, the names and dates of birth of any children, present address. In the case of yourself, all these things will be known to you from memory, but you should support them with as much documentation as possible. When you write up the pages relating to your parents, grandparents and great-grandparents, most of your information will come from the results of your researches, and will also include the date and place of death. The longer they lived, the more information you should have. These notes will form the bare branches on which the leaves will grow.

The following is a copy of the first notes made relating to a member of my family whom I knew and who was able personally to give me many details on which to base my researches. It is therefore recent history:

Fanny Rayner (A1)
Born: 7 May 1896, Bilgoraj, Poland
Parents: Maurice Rayner (A3), Esther? (M36)
Schools: Hackney Primary, Green's Grammar School, Stepney.
Residence: 306 Wick Road, Hackney
Occupation: hairdresser
Married: 18 October 1926 Hackney Register Office
Alfred Gennings (S4) – Occupation: Engineer
Present: Rebecca Gosman and William Edward Gennings (S7) (Groom's brother)
Female child born 3 October 1928 Elizabeth Esther (S12)
Residences: 1926–1929 21 Greenwood Road, Hackney
1930–1940 91 Farley Road, Stoke Newington
1941–1949 9 Wellington Road, Leyton
1950–1965 33 Naverino Road, Hackney
1966–1979 18 Kirkstead Court, Hackney
Died: 21 November 1979

All the necessary facts are there, but how bleak and uninteresting. The following is the beginning of the rounded history of Fanny Rayner:

'Fanny Rayner, the daughter of Maurice and Esther, was born in Bilgoraj, Poland, on 7 May 1896. The maiden name of Esther is not known since no birth certificate is known to exist for Fanny but an Affidavit sworn by her father in January 1956 gives the details of her birth. Maurice and Esther, with Fanny, emigrated to England in 1900.

The family lived at 306 Wick Road in a prosperous part of the London Borough of Hackney over the hairdresser's establishment opened by Maurice where he catered for the local population, both men and women. The shop was well situated between a public house and a grocer's store, close to Victoria Park, in an area comprising both shopping and residential accommodation. Fanny attended the local primary school and gained a scholarship to Sir George Green's Grammar School in Stepney. She remained at the school until the age of 16 and then joined her father in his shop as an apprentice hairdresser. Fanny was 5ft 2in tall, had dark hair and brown eyes. At the age of 28 years on 18 October 1926, Fanny married Alfred Gennings, an engineer, of 9 Etropol Road, Hackney. The witnesses to the marriage were Rebecca Gosman, a friend of Fanny, and William Edward Gennings, Alfred's younger brother. Fanny ceased her occupation as a hairdresser and took up residence with her husband Alfred in rented accommodation at 21 Greenwood Road, Hackney where they were living when her only child, a daughter, Elizabeth Esther was born at the Mothers' Hospital in Hackney on 3 October 1928. Elizabeth Esther weighing only 4½ lb at birth was born prematurely and Fanny was unable to have any more children.

Fanny remained at home looking after her family while Alfred continued to work as an engineer. They moved house in 1930 to 91 Farley Road, Stoke Newington, once again in rented accommodation. Fanny became a voluntary school assistant in 1935 at Upton House School, Hackney and a School Governor in 1937. In 1939 she assisted with the evacuation of the children f Upton House School to Thetford in Norfolk, where she nained for a year acting as a liaison between the children, parents and the local population. Later she returned to

London to work in a munitions factory . . .' and so the story continues until her death in 1979.

The story is Fanny's with references to her father, mother, daughter and brother-in-law. Her parents Maurice and Esther each have their own page and story, as do her husband Alfred and her daughter Elizabeth Esther. Elizabeth Esther's children and grandchildren also make an appearance further on in the saga. Fanny's story is by no means complete. You will have noticed that there is a gap between her age at 16 and at 28. Other parts of her early life are only sketched in with the information at present known. There is a need for much more research. So it always will be with family history and genealogy – a never ending journey.

The documents supporting this part of the family history are the original Affidavit of her father, three school reports, a photograph of Fanny standing on the doorstep of her father's shop. Her original marriage certificate, letters written from Thetford in Norfolk, a photograph of a group of factory munition workers, and her death certificate. You may notice that Fanny's date of birth of May 1896 does not agree with her age at her marriage. Perhaps her father was mistaken about her date of birth or the incorrect age was entered on her marriage certificate. This is just one example of the inconsistencies that you may find as you research your family history.

The following are brief extracts from manuscripts written by a family historian in 1850 which were given to me as part of the family documentation of a family for whom I prepared a family history. The style of writing is very different from that used today and very little detail is given, but the writer conveys to the reader his sensitivity and the tender feelings he still held for his deceased wife. The first and second refer to one of his relations and the third, although apparently written from a distance, to his own wife.

'Angus Bantry son of Jonathan Bantry a yeoman of Eden End, Northamptonshire and grandson of Samuel Bantry was sent to Highcroft school with the idea of being a farmer, but not liking it, and farming being bad, he came to Manchester as a boy of fifteen with ten shillings in his pocket and obtained a post in a bank and became rich.'

The second by Angus himself refers to a letter he received from a clergyman.

'This letter from Rev Mr Tree the clergyman then residing at Eden End was written about the 12th January 1808 and the half guinea enclosed to me was all my capital for starting life. Before my good father left me in Manchester he gave me a five pound note because at that time I had no salary from the Banking House and to the best of my recollection I never received further assistance from him or any one else.'

The third written by Daniel Bantry.

'Alice, the beloved wife of Daniel Bantry, was the eldest daughter of Thomas and Nancy Harding and was born at their house in Manchester on March 22nd 1793. She was married on April 9th 1817 and soon afterwards attended at Chapel and was with her husband baptised June 30th 1821. Eighteen years before her decease her growing afflictions prevented her from regular attendance on the means of grace and for the last ten years of her life she was almost entirely confined to her habitation. She suffered most patiently from what was supposed to be a heart disease and died on November 3rd 1850. She was buried in Oldham cemetery in a family grave which is indicated by a neat marble monument.'

These pages, including the one from my own family history, give you an idea of how to begin writing your family history. Develop your own style and add to your manuscripts as your research progresses.

With the aid of the internet, software programs and the use of photographs scanned into your PC, you can produce a very professional family history. A number of companies now offer to print digitally a short run (something like 25 copies) and bind family histories with a printed cover for a reasonable cost. These companies advertise in family history magazines.

Having conveyed to you the enjoyment and pleasure that can be derived from the pursuit of family history, I wish you success and leave you to draw up your own tree. There are many elements of family history research that I have not dealt with and some that have been mentioned only in passing. Inevitably you will have many questions you would like to ask. There is more detailed information relating to the IGI, museums and The National Archives and I am conscious of the fact that I have not dealt with how to find your ancestors if they were originally immigrants or if they emigrated. I am sure, however, that I have given you more than enough to whet your appetite and keep you occupied, and your own researches will lead you to many answers.

One more thing before we part company. I realize I have made the point many times, but record offices, museums and repositories do change their hours of opening and sometimes have to close for stocktaking, conservation or redecoration. Please do telephone in advance to check times and availability of records so as to avoid a wasted journey.

The internet will also give you valuable information regarding addresses and opening times.

APPENDIX

Useful names and addresses, telephone numbers, websites and hours of opening (all liable to change with the passage of time). Be aware of bank holiday variations.

Chapter 1: Looking For Your Ancestors

The National Archives website
www.nationalarchives.gov.uk

The Society of Genealogists website
www.sog.org.uk

FindMyPast website
www.findmypast.com

Ancestry website
www.ancestry.co.uk

FreeBMD website
www.freebmd.org.uk

Genes Reunited website
www.GenesReunited.co.uk

Open University website
www.open.ac.uk

**Chapter 2: Birth, Marriage and Death Certificates
(England and Wales)**
The General Register Office (GRO) website
www.gro.gov.uk/gro/content/certificates

Online applications:
Cost of full certificate with exact GRO reference: £7.
Cost of full certificate without GRO reference: £10

Postal applications to:
General Register Office
PO Box 2
Southport
Merseyside
PR8 2JD
Made payable to ONS.

Or order by telephone with a debit or credit card: 0845 603
7788.
Or order by fax with a debit or credit card: 01704 550013
Cost of standard certificate with exact GRO reference: £8.50.
Cost of standard certificate without GRO reference: £11.50.

Information on Adoptions at
http://www.gro.gov.uk/gro/content/adoptions/index.asp

Chapter 3: Birth, Marriage and Death Certificates (Elsewhere in the UK, the Isle of Man and the Channel Islands)

General Register Office (Scotland)
New Register House
3 West Register Street
Edinburgh
EH1 3YT
Tel: 0131 334 0380
www.gro-scotland.gov.uk

Opening times:
Monday to Friday: 9 am to 4.30 pm.
Closed: Saturday, Sunday and some bank holidays.
Appointment necessary.
Search fees:
Daily: £17.
Afternoon only (unbookable): £10.
Weekly: £65.
Four-weekly: £220.
Yearly: £1,500.

The official government source of genealogical data for Scotland
www.scotlandspeople.gov.uk

Strathclyde Area Genealogy Centre
22 Park Circus
Glasgow
G3 6BE
Tel: 0141 287 8364
www.glasgow.gov.uk/en/Visitors/FamilyHistory
Opening times:
Monday to Friday: 9.30 am to 4 pm.
Daily search fee.
Appointment necessary.

General Register Office (Ireland)
Postal address:
General Register Office
Government Offices
Convent Road
Roscommon
Republic of Ireland

Research Room:
3rd Floor, Block 7
Irish Life Centre
Lower Abbey Street
Dublin 1
Republic of Ireland
Tel: 00 353 90 6632900
Fax: 00 353 90 6632999
www.groireland.ie

Opening times:
Monday to Friday 9.30 am to 4.30 pm (excluding bank holidays).
Search fees:
Daily: 20 Euros.
One search for 5 years: 2 Euros.
Photocopies: 4 Euros.

General Register Office (Northern Ireland)
Oxford House
49-55 Chichester Street
Belfast
BT1 4HL
Northern Ireland
Tel: 028 9025 2000
www.groni.gov.uk

Opening times:
Monday to Friday: 9.30 am to 4 pm (excluding bank holidays).
No entrance fee charged.

Isle of Man General Registry
Deemsters Walk
Buck's Road
Douglas
Isle of Man
IM1 3AR
Tel: 01624 687039
www.gov.im/infocentre

Opening times:
Monday to Friday: 9 am to 5 pm.
Closed: Lunch daily 1 pm to 2 pm, Sunday, bank holidays.
No entrance fee charged.

Superintendent Registrar
States Building
10 Royal Square
St Helier
Jersey
JE2 4WA
Tel: 01534 502335

The Société Jersiaise
Lord Coutanche Library
7 Pier Road
St Helier
Jersey
JE2 4XW
Tel: 01534 730538
www.societe-jersiaise.org

Opening times:
Monday to Friday: 9 am to 5 pm.

Jersey Archive
Clarence Road
St Helier
Jersey
JE2 4JY
Tel: 01534 833333
www.jerseyheritagetrust.org

Opening times:
Tuesday to Saturday: 9 am to 1 pm, 2 pm to 5 pm.

Registrar General
The Greffe
Royal Court House
St Peter Port
Guernsey
GY1 2PB
Tel: 01481 725277

Opening times for searches:
Monday to Friday: 2 pm to 4 pm.
Search fee of £1 payable.

Cost of each certificate applied for in person: £5.
A minimum charge of £5 is made for a search of the birth, marriage and death registers requested by post.

Priaulx Library
Candie Road
St Peter Port
Guernsey
GY1 1UG
Tel: 01481 721998
www.priaulxlibrary.gov.gg

Chapter 4: Keeping Your Records
PC programs, shareware, CD-Rom and binder suppliers:
S & N Genealogy Supplies (Mail Order)
West Wing
Manor Farm
Chilmark
Salisbury
Wiltshire
SP3 5AF
Tel: 01722 716121
www.GenealogySupplies.com

Genealogical Storage website for binders and acid-free pockets
www.cwsparkinson.co.uk

Chapter 6: Where Do We Go From Here?

Association of Genealogists and Researchers in Archives (AGRA)
Joint Secretaries
29 Badgers Close
Horsham
West Sussex
RH12 5RU
www.agra.org.uk

Association of Professional Genealogists
PO Box 350998
Westminster
CO 80035-0998
USA
www.apgen.org
email: admin@apgen.org

Stephen T J Wright
London Research Service
4 Rose Glen
Chelmsford
CM2 9EN
Tel: 01245 259965
www.LondonResearchService.com

Chapter 7: Census Returns
Ancestry website
www.ancestry.co.uk

1901 census website
www.1901census.nationalarchives.gov.uk

FindMyPast website
www.findmypast.com

LDS Family Search website
www.familysearch.org

S & N Genealogy Supplies website
www.GenealogySupplies.com

ScotlandsPeople website
www.scotlandspeople.gov.uk

National Archives of Ireland
Bishop Street
Dublin 8
Eire
Tel: 00 353 1 407 2300
www.nationalarchives.ie
www.census.nationalarchives.ie

Opening times:
Monday to Friday: 10 am to 5 pm.
Closed: Saturday, Sunday, bank holidays.

Manx National Heritage Library
Douglas
Isle of Man
IM1 3LY
Tel: 01624 648000
www.gov.im/mnh

Jersey Public Library
Halkett Place
St Helier
Jersey
JE2 4WH
Tel: 01534 448701
www.jsylib.gov.je
Personal visits are preferred.

1911 census website
www.nationalarchives.gov.uk/1911census

Chapter 8: Parish Registers
GENUKI website
www.genuki.org.uk

The Genealogist website
www.thegenealogist.co.uk

British Origins website
www.originsnetwork.com

National Library of Wales
Aberystwyth
Ceredigion
SY23 3BU
Tel: 01970 632800
www.llgc.org.uk

Catholic Family History Society
www.catholic-history.org.uk/cfhs

Catholic National Library
St Michael's Abbey
Farnborough Road
Farnborough
Hampshire
GU14 7NQ
Tel: 01252 543818
www.catholic-library.org.uk

Jewish Museum
Raymond Burton House
129-131 Albert Street
Camden Town
London
NW1 7NB
Tel: 020 7284 1997
www.jewishmuseum.org.uk

At the time of writing, the museum is closed while undertaking a major transformation project. It is planned to reopen in 2009.

Library of the Society of Friends
Friends House
173 Euston Road
London
NW1 2BJ
Tel: 020 7663 1135
Fax: 020 7663 1001

www.quaker.org.uk/library/index.html
email: library@quaker.org.uk
Contacting the library in advance of your visit is advised.

Baptist Historical Society website
www.baptisthistory.org.uk

Methodist Archives and Research Centre
John Rylands University Library of Manchester
Oxford Road
Manchester
M13 9PP
Tel: 0161 275 3751
www.library.manchester.ac.uk/specialcollections/
collections/methodist

Huguenot Library (postal address)
University Library
Gower Street
London
WC1E 6BT
Tel: 020 7679 5199
Appointment necessary.
www.huguenotsociety.org.uk
The library is housed within the Special Collections of UCL
Library, 140 Hampstead Road, London, NW1.

National Library, Dublin
Kildare Street
Dublin 2
Eire
Tel: 00 353 1 603 0200
www.nli.ie

Irish Times, Irish Ancestors website
www.ireland.com/ancestor

From Ireland website
www.from-ireland.net

Public Record Office of Northern Ireland
66 Balmoral Avenue
Belfast
BT9 6NY
www.proni.gov.uk

Chapter 9: Wills, Probate and Monumental Inscriptions
Principal Probate Registry
First Avenue House
42-49 High Holborn
London
WC1V 6NP
Tel: 020 7947 7022
www.courtservice.gov.uk/cms/wills.htm

The Postal Searches and Copies Department
The Probate Registry
Castle Chambers
Clifford Street
York
YO1 9RG
Tel: 01904 666777

National Archives of Scotland
H M General Register House
2 Princes Street
Edinburgh
EH1 3YY
Tel: 0131 535 1334 (Historical Search Room)
Tel: 0131 535 1413 (West Search Room)
www.nas.gov.uk

Scottish Archive Network
Thomas Thomson House
99 Bankhead Crossway North
Edinburgh
EH11 4DX
www.scottishdocuments.com

Irish Origins website
www.irishorigins.com

Chapter 10: The National Archives
The National Archives
Ruskin Avenue
Kew
Richmond
Surrey
TW9 4DU
Tel: 020 8876 3444
www.nationalarchives.gov.uk

Opening times:
Monday and Friday: 9 am to 5 pm.
Tuesday: 9 am to 7 pm.

Wednesday: 10 am to 5 pm.
Thursday: 9 am to 7 pm.
Saturday: 9.30 am to 5 pm.
Closed: Sunday and bank holidays, first week in December for stocktaking.
Reader's ticket required – no charge.
Copying service.

Documents Online
www.nationalarchives.gov.uk/documentsonline

AncestorsOnBoard website
www.ancestorsonboard.com

London Gazette website
www.gazettesonline.co.uk

Police websites
www.policeorders.co.uk
www.met.police.uk/history

The British Postal Museum and Archives
Freeling House
Phoenix Place
London
WC1X 0DL
Tel: 020 7239 2570
www.postalheritage.org.uk

Chapter 11: More Sources for Research

Cyndi's List website
www.cyndislist.com

GENUKI website
www.genuki.org.uk

ARCHON website
www.nationalarchives.gov.uk/archon

Access to Archives website
www.nationalarchives.gov.uk/a2a

Commonwealth War Graves website
www.cwgc.org

Saga's website
www.saga.co.uk

The Church of Jesus Christ of Latter-day Saints
Website for the IGI, Ancestral file and some census information. More records to be added:
www.familysearch.com

Teletext
Family Tree
PO Box 297
London
SW6 1XT

Postcards or one page fax only.
Include your own name and address.
www.teletext.co.uk/news

Army Personnel Centre
Historical Disclosures
Mail Point 555
Kentigern House
65 Brown Street
Glasgow
G2 8EX
http://www.veterans-uk.info/service_records/army.html

Navy Records
RN Disclosures Cell
Room 48
West Battery
Whale Island
Portsmouth
Hampshire
PO2 8DX
http://www.veterans-uk.info/service_records/royal_navy.html

RAF Records
RAF Disclosures Section
Room 221b
Trenchard Hall
RAF Cranwell
Sleaford
Lincolnshire
NG34 8HB
http://www.veterans-uk.info/service_records/raf.html

Chapter 12: Libraries and Research Centres

Society of Genealogists
14 Charterhouse Buildings
Goswell Road
London
EC1M 7BA
Tel: 020 7251 8799
www.sog.org.uk

Opening times:
Tuesday, Wednesday, Friday, Saturday: 10 am to 6 pm.
Thursday: 10 am to 8 pm.
Closed: Monday, bank holidays, one week in February.
Search fees:
£4 per hour.
£10 for 4 hours.
£18 per day.
No fees for members.

Guildhall Library
Aldermanbury
London
EC2P 2EJ
Tel: 020 7332 1868
www.cityoflondon.gov.uk

London Metropolitan Archives
40 Northampton Road
London
EC1R 0HB
Tel: 020 7332 3820
www.cityoflondon.gov.uk

Federation of Family History Societies website
www.ffhs.org.uk

GOONS (Guild of One Name Studies) website
www.one-name.org

Borthwick Institute of Historical Research
University of York
Heslington
York
YO10 5DD
Tel: 01904 321166
www.york.ac.uk/inst/bihr

Copying facilities.
Appointment necessary. Ring to book one.

British Library Newspaper Library
Colindale Avenue
London
NW9 5HE
Tel: 020 7412 7353
www.bl.uk/collections/newspapers.html

Opening times:
Monday to Saturday: 10 am to 5 pm.
Closed: Sunday, bank holidays.
Copying facilities.
Reader's ticket required. No charges.

Oriental and India Office Collections
British Library
96 Euston Road
London
NW1 2DB
Tel: 020 7412 7873
www.bl.uk/collections/orientalandindian.html

Reading Room opening times:
Monday: 10 am to 5 pm.
Tuesday to Saturday: 9.30 am to 5 pm.
Closed: Sunday, bank holidays.

Reader's pass required. Valid either 1 month or 5 years.

India Family website
http://indiafamily.bl.uk/UI

National Coal Mining Museum
Caphouse Colliery
New Road
Overton
Wakefield
WF4 4RH
Tel: 01924 848806
www.ncm.org.uk

Morpeth Chantry Bagpipe Museum
Bridge Street
Morpeth
Northumberland
NE61 1PD
Tel: 01670 500717

Museum of Chartered Insurance Institute
20 Aldermanbury
London
EC2V 7HY

St Bride Library
Bride Lane
Fleet Street
London
EC4Y 8EE
Tel: 020 7353 4660
www.stbride.org/

QUICK INDEX TO USEFUL WEBSITES

This is a short list of the websites referred to in this book which I hope you will find useful as you research your family history. Be aware that addresses can change over time. There are, of course, many more sites on the internet which may be able to help you, and new sites come online every month. However, always make sure you check out the background of any website before parting with any money for any goods or services.

Access to Archives: www.nationalarchives.gov.uk/a2a
Adoptions:
   http://www.gro.gov.uk/gro/content/adoptions/index.asp
AncestorsOnBoard: www.ancestorsonboard.com
Ancestry: www.ancestry.co.uk
ARCHON: www.nationalarchives.gov.uk/archon
Army Records: http://www.veterans-uk.info/service_records/
   army.html
Baptist Historical Society: www.baptisthistory.org.uk
Borthwick Institute: www.york.ac.uk/inst/bihr
British Origins: www.originsnetwork.com
Catholic Family History Society:
   www.catholic-history.org.uk/cfhs
Catholic National Library: www.catholic-library.org.uk

Census (1901): www.1901census.nationalarchives.gov.uk
Census (1911): www.nationalarchives.gov.uk/1911census
Coal Mining Museum: www.ncm.org.uk
Commonwealth War Graves: www.cwgc.org
Cyndi's List: www.cyndislist.com
Documents Online:
   www.nationalarchives.gov.uk/documentsonline
Federation of Family History Societies: www.ffhs.org.uk
FindMyPast: www.findmypast.com
FreeBMD: www.freebmd.org.uk
Genealogical Storage: www.cwsparkinson.co.uk
The Genealogist: www.thegenealogist.co.uk
General Register Office:
   www.gro.gov.uk/gro/content/certificates
Genes Reunited: www.GenesReunited.co.uk
GENUKI: www.genuki.org.uk
Guild of One Name Studies: www.one-name.org
Guildhall Library: www.cityoflondon.gov.uk
Huguenot Library: www.huguenotsociety.org.uk
India Family: http://indiafamily.bl.uk/UI
India Office: www.bl.uk/collections/orientalandindian.html
Ireland: Census: www.census.nationalarchives.ie
Ireland: General Register Office: www.groireland.ie
Ireland: National Archives: www.nationalarchives.ie
Ireland: National Library: www.nli.ie
From Ireland: www.from-ireland.net
Irish Ancestors: www.ireland.com/ancestor
Irish Origins: www.irishorigins.com
Isle of Man General Registry: www.gov.im/infocentre
Jersey Archive: www.jerseyheritagetrust.org
Jersey Public Library: www.jsylib.gov.je
Jersey: Société Jersiaise: www.societe-jersiaise.org
Jewish Museum: www.jewishmuseum.org.uk
LDS Family Search: www.familysearch.org
London Gazette: www.gazettesonline.co.uk

London Metropolitan Archives: www.cityoflondon.gov.uk
London Research Service:
  www.LondonResearchService.com
Manx National Heritage Library: www.gov.im/mnh
Methodist Archives: www.library.manchester.ac.uk/special-
  collections/collections/methodist
National Archives: www.nationalarchives.gov.uk
Navy Records: http://www.veterans-uk.info/service_
  records/royal_navy.html
Newspaper Library:
  www.bl.uk/collections/newspapers.html
Northern Ireland General Register Office:
  www.groni.gov.uk
Northern Ireland: Public Record Office: www.proni.gov.uk
Open University: www.open.ac.uk
Police: www.policeorders.co.uk
Police: www.met.police.uk/history
Postal Archives: www.postalheritage.org.uk
Priaulx Library: www.priaulxlibrary.gov.gg
Professional Genealogists (AGRA): www.agra.org.uk
Professional Genealogists (APG): www.apgen.org
RAF Records:
  http://www.veterans-uk.info/service_records/raf.html
S & N Genealogy Supplies: www.GenealogySupplies.com
Saga: www.saga.co.uk
Scotland: General Register Office:
  www.gro-scotland.gov.uk
Scotland: Glasgow Centre:
  www.glasgow.gov.uk/en/Visitors/FamilyHistory
Scotland: National Archives: www.nas.gov.uk
Scotlands People: www.scotlandspeople.gov.uk
Scottish Archive Network: www.scottishdocuments.com
Society of Friends library:
  www.quaker.org.uk/library/index.html
Society of Genealogists: www.sog.org.uk

St Bride Library: www.stbride.org/
Teletext: www.teletext.co.uk/news
Wales: National Library: www.llgc.org.uk
Wills and Probate: www.courtservice.gov.uk/cms/wills.htm

INDEX

To order these Right Way titles please fill in the form below

No. of copies	Title	Price	Total
	How to Solve Cryptic Crosswords	£4.99	
	The Curry Secret	£5.99	
	For P&P add £2.50 for the first book, £1 for each additional book		
	Grand Total		£

Name: _____

Address:_____

_____ Postcode: _____

Daytime Tel. No./Email _____
(in case of query)

Three ways to pay:
1. Telephone the TBS order line on 01206 255 800.
   Order lines are open Monday – Friday, 8:30am–5:30pm.
2. I enclose a cheque made payable to **TBS Ltd** for £_____
3. Please charge my ☐ Visa ☐ Mastercard ☐ Amex
   ☐ Maestro (issue no. _____)

Card number:_____

Expiry date: _____ Last three digits on back of card:_____

Signature: _____
(your signature is essential when paying by credit or debit card)

**Please return forms to Cash Sales/Direct Mail Dept.,
The Book Service, Colchester Road, Frating Green,
Colchester CO7 7DW.**

Enquiries to readers@constablerobinson.com.

Constable and Robinson Ltd (directly or via its agents)
may mail, email or phone you about promotions or products.

☐ Tick box if you do not want these from us ☐ or our subsidiaries.

**www.right-way.co.uk
www.constablerobinson.com**